£1·99

RUGBY

An Anthology

RUGBY

An Anthology

The Brave, the Bruised and the Brilliant

COMPILED BY

BRIAN LEVISON

ROBINSON

ROBINSON

First published in Great Britain in 2015 by Robinson

A CIP catalogue record for this book
is available from the British Library.

ISBN 978-1-47213-571-1 (paperback)
ISBN: 978-1-47213-572-8 (ebook)

Typeset in Adobe Caslon by SX Composing DTP, Rayleigh, Essex
Printed and bound in Great Britain by CPI (UK) Ltd, Croydon CR0 4YY

Papers used by Robinson are from well-managed forests and
other responsible sources

MIX
Paper from
responsible sources
FSC® C104740

Robinson
An imprint of
Little, Brown Book Group
Carmelite House
50 Victoria Embankment
London EC4Y 0DZ

An Hachette UK Company
www.hachette.co.uk

www.littlebrown.co.uk

To Jill with love

Contents

4

THE HARD MEN

5

THE WHISTLE BLOWERS

6

BEYOND THE TOUCHLINE

7

GIVING IT EVERYTHING

8

TIME OFF

9

DOUBLE VISION

10

FLIERS AND DODGERS

Foreword

J. P. R. WILIAMS

It is a great honour and privilege to write a foreword to *Rugby: An Anthology*.

The history of the game is fascinating in that I, like many others, assumed that William Webb Ellis founded the game at Rugby School in 1823.

The game of rugby union has changed greatly over the years, even since the amateur days of mine to the professional days of today. However, I feel the ethos of the game has survived. It is a very physical game but still has the enjoyment that players and spectators love so much.

Yes, the game today does not have the social side as much as in the Old Days, but there is still the chance to meet your opponent for a chat (perhaps an apology) after the game. This I think is the best thing about the game and helps to prevent long term vendettas.

The many contributors to this anthology have covered all aspects of the game and there are some great stories. All in all an excellent rugby book and one which every keen supporter should have on his shelf.

Introduction

BRIAN LEVISON

'THE RUGBY PLAYER during the course of a game is living life at its most intoxicating. There is movement, energy, grace, strength, fear, intelligence, competition, everything,' Rowe Harding writes in the final piece of this book. Add humour and this would seem about as comprehensive a definition of rugby as you can get, though no doubt other games and sports will argue that it also applies to them.

In the thirteen sections of this selection, these qualities will appear many times. 'In the Beginning' takes a none-too-serious look at the history and pre-history of rugby and touches on the shape of the ball with a member of the Gilbert family, as well as players' clothing, the origin of some of the rules, and Sue Mott's witty definition of the playing positions seen from a woman's perspective. 'Invocations' pays due deference to the Haka and gives it a place of honour at the start of the book as in any game involving the All Blacks, though Brian O'Driscoll voices some reservations. International and senior club rugby attracts most of the public and press attention, but there are those who know they will never become first team players and simply play 'For the Love of It'. To judge from Stephen Gauge and Richard Beard, they have a very enjoyable time.

'The Hard Men' investigates the dark arts of the pack, and introduces us to big beasts like Jean 'Le Sultan' Sébédio, Blair Swannell and Roger McGough's Big Arth (from Penarth). 'The Whistle Blowers' takes a behind-the-scenes look at the involvement of the referee, particularly the often amusing and informal interaction behind him and the players with contributions from, among others, Derek Bevan, Brian Moore and a Pontypool perspective from Nick Bishop and Alun Carter. 'Beyond the Touchline' looks at the impact of events off the field. Phil Vickery explains the importance to him of the passionate Gloucester crowd, and Chris Laidlaw introduces New Zealand's most famous supporter, Little Eric from Berhampore. The great All Black full-back George Nepia tells what he owed to some unorthodox healing methods.

In many pieces, a player will say 'we gave it everything'. 'Giving It Everything' is something rugby players conspicuously did on the battlefield too, as starkly described by Tony Collins's 'The War Game' and Mick Imlah's poem 'London Scottish (1914)'. 'Time Off' provides a little light reading to keep yourself amused during the dead time while the referee and TMO (television match official) take ages to decide what is perfectly clear to any supporter, depending on the decision you want. It is said that there are two sides to every story and 'Double Vision' takes four incidents and gives you the differing points of view of two of those involved. Among the pairings are Willie John McBride against Colin Meads, and Graham Mourie at odds with J. P. R. Williams.

'Fliers and Dodgers' looks at some of the great three-quarter and half-backs such as Gerald Davies and Peter Jackson. You will not find much in the history books about the English scrum-half Rev. Matthew Mullineux (*c*.1900), but the poem by the Australian 'Banjo' Patterson gives a very graphic impression of him, one of three poems in this section, as backs seem to inspire more poetry than forwards. 'Tight Heads and Loose Forwards' concentrates less on specialists in these positions and more on the tight and loose aspects of post-match activities with the experienced help of Jeff Probyn, Jean-Pierre Rives and W. W. Wakefield among others. 'Last Line of Defence' completes the team and looks at the most highly-regarded full-backs such as George Nepia, J. P. R. Williams and Gavin Hastings. Finally, 'No-side', is called. A. A. Thomson and John Dann write evocatively about their passion for rugby and its place in their lives.

Contributors include some of the best-known names of rugby, like Brian O'Driscoll, Willie John McBride, Gavin Hastings, Graham Mourie, Brian Moore, Phil Vickery, George Nepia, Chris Laidlaw, Chester Williams, Colin Deans, Eddie Butler, J. P. R. Williams and Jeff Probyn. Among the respected writers, historians and commentators are Sir Terry McLean, E. H. D. Sewell, Howard Marshall, Robert Lynd, Frank Keating, Alec Waugh, Chris Greyvenstein, J. B. G. Thomas, John Reason and Carwyn James.

I am very grateful to Jill Haas and Matthew Levison for their considerable help and suggestions. Thanks also to the staff of the library at the World Rugby Museum, Twickenham Stadium, and to the staff of the Bodleian Library.

Brian Levison
Oxford

1

IN THE BEGINNING

In the Beginning, Long Before 1823 . . .

JOHN REASON AND CARWYN JAMES

In modern times, the idea that rugby originated when William Webb Ellis
picked up and ran with the ball in 1823 is the exception rather than the rule.
Rugby journalist John Reason and former British and Irish Lions' and
Llanelli coach Carwyn James set out the current received view in
The World of Rugby: A History of Rugby Union Football (1979).

THE STORY ABOUT William Webb Ellis has never sounded very convincing.
It is hard to believe that hundreds of boys at Rugby School suddenly cried
'Eureka', stopped what they had been doing for years and did something else,
simply because one unexceptional and somewhat reluctant young footballer
broke the rules of the game as it was played at the school in 1823.

If you believe the story, and accept this version of the manufacture of
instant rugby football, you will believe, without question, the inscription on
the stone tablet which is built into the wall between Rugby School and what
is still one of its playing fields. The inscription reads:

> This stone commemorates the exploit of William Webb Ellis, who
> with a fine disregard for the rules of football as played in his time,
> first took the ball in his arms and ran with it, thus originating the
> distinctive feature of the Rugby Game.

However, at a time when George IV was still early in his reign, and a man
could still be hung for sheep-stealing, it is pushing credibility to suggest that
any disregard of rules could ever be looked upon as 'fine' by contemporary
society. It is also quite untrue to say that picking the ball up and running with
it was a 'distinctive feature of the Rugby Game', because it had been a feature
of football since time immemorial.

Even the suggestion that William Webb Ellis was the first to do it at Rugby School takes some swallowing, because the only historical evidence to support this assertion is contained in a letter written to a magazine more than fifty years after the alleged event, and the letter was no more than hearsay. What is more, it was immediately refuted by a schoolboy contemporary of Ellis, who wrote: 'I remember William Webb Ellis perfectly. He was an admirable cricketer, but was generally regarded as inclined to take unfair advantages at football. I should not quote him in any way as an authority.'

This hardly sounds the stuff of which trail-blazers are made, and although it may be thoroughly disrespectful and even sacrilegious to say so, it is difficult to escape the conclusion that when William Webb Ellis picked up the ball it was already part of the game at the school, because it certainly was not an innovation. It may even be true, as has been suggested, that he was running away from the opposition rather than at them, though we would not go as far as those cheerful disparagers who dismiss young Master Ellis as both a coward and a cheat!

Whatever the truth of the matter, it is a good story. All legends are, and no doubt it will be, faithfully recounted in some suitable pamphlet to be read by endless American tourists when Rugby School takes its place on the summer circuit leading to Stratford-upon-Avon just up the road.

... Not that the school is under any illusions about the William Webb Ellis legend. When the filming for *The World of Rugby* television series was taking place, Malcolm Lee acknowledged the doubts of the sceptics.

'There is very little evidence to support the popular belief that William Webb Ellis created a new form of football,' he said. 'The point is that the rules of the game as it was played at the school at that time were made by the boys themselves and those rules were constantly revised. If you look at the notes of the Big Side Levees – notes made by the boys themselves – you will see that the rules were discussed almost every time the boys went out to play and that adjustments were frequently made.'

Perhaps we should point out that despite its overtones of Mississippi *franglais*, a Big Side Levee was not a riverside embankment on the estate of the local Al Capone, but simply a meeting of interested parties on the field at the side of the Big School where most of the teaching was done and where Doctor Arnold and Tom Brown went their various ways.

The notes of these meetings were written by the boys, and the books in which they were written were not even seen by the masters until one book had been filled and the next one was in the process of compilation. These books are still preserved at the school, and in the careful handwriting of the students of the time, various delightful playing conditions were recorded. One reads: 'At a Big Side Levee held on Tuesday, September 12, 1848, it was agreed that ... for this year, the Sixth Match to last for Five Days or for Seven Days if a goal be kicked, instead of Three and Five respectively as heretofore ...'

This constant revision of the rules was common to most of the public schools at that time. They all played their own forms of football and as often as not it involved most of the boys in the school. Sketches of games played in the early nineteenth century reveal that the two teams were hardly ever equal in number and anything up to a hundred a side. Boys of all ages and consequently vastly different physiques took part, and most of them seemed to have been there just for the age-old pleasure of competing for possession of a ball and achieving a goal, with the added satisfaction of being expressly permitted to kick each other in the process!

Certainly, rugby football was not evolved in the space of a wet weekend, as the game of lawn tennis was by the celebrated Major Wingfield, or as the game of badminton was by two bored guests at the Duke of Badminton's estate in the West Country.

The evolution of the different codes of football was much slower. The people living in Victorian Britain were the most energetic and inventive since the Romans, but football was too deeply rooted in history to be susceptible to the sort of dramatic change suggested by that stone tablet at Rugby School. If you watch children playing a game of their own invention, or adaptation, you will see that it is inconceivable that rugby football should have been produced like a great blinding light suddenly shining forth. When children play a game, perhaps the most noticeable feature is that they invariably make it up as they go along, partly by experiment, partly by argument and partly by invention. It is a slow process and the essential point about the different games of football played at the public schools at that time was that they all *were* games developed by the boys themselves.

There was nothing new about football, of course. That had been played for at least 2,000 years. There was nothing new about picking up the ball and running with it, either. That had been the essence of the game throughout its history. Indeed, if you study the history of football you will see that the one truly remarkable thing about rugby football is *not* that it is a new game but that it is precisely the opposite, because it is the football which most closely resembles that played from before the time of the Romans and right through the Middle Ages. The real innovators were those footballers at schools like Eton, who wanted just to kick the ball, rather than pick it up and run with it, because they disapproved of the sweatily violent exercises such as hacking and mauling, though no doubt even they would have shut their eyes in horror if they had seen the lack of physical challenge and hurly burly in the game of Association football as it is played now. The boys at Rugby School simply defended the faith, probably unconsciously, and stuck broadly to the game played by their forefathers.

❧

The Evolution of Rugby

FRANK C. HAWKINS AND E. SEYMOUR-BELL

According to the authors, the direct antecedent of modern rugby is a game
played in Italy in the sixteenth century. From *Fifty Years with the
Clifton Rugby Football Club* (1922).

❧

THE QUESTION IS often asked, 'How, when and where did rugby first come into being?' Writers have recorded that a game known as 'Harpastum' was played in the days of Julius Caesar. Apparently in this game one set of players (there is no record of the positions they held on the field of play, neither are the numbers given) used to strive to carry a ball through the territory held by their opponents, and although a highly imaginative person could make this into a game of rugby there is not enough detail to decide whether it was the true origin.

In England a few centuries ago Shrove Tuesday used to be set aside for a queer sort of game in which whole parishes were matched against one another. Commencing in the market place with partisans of each parish lined up, a large ball was tossed into the midst of them, and it then became the object of each party to impel their opponents towards their particular goal – a jolly good scrum maybe, but hardly rugger.

Fry's Magazine, now defunct, once had an interesting article on an Italian game 'Il Calcio' played in the sixteenth century, and it is more than probable that rugby footballers have to thank Florentine athletes for the invention of the game and for its introduction into this country. Only those of noble or gentle blood, or such as had gained distinction or rank in the profession of arms, were allowed to participate in 'Il Calcio': while each player had to be of unblemished reputation, of graceful figure, and possessed of accomplished manners. With teams comprising such models of virtue surely the referee, or umpire as he was then termed, could not have had quite so difficult a task as some of our officials today. The players would create quite a stir in these times were they to appear as then dressed; for a Clifton fifteen to wear tunics of silk with feathered caps all richly embroidered in gold and silver, tight-fitting drawers, and shoes of leather and silver, would certainly draw a 'gate' to say the least. The numbers participating in this game varied according to the size of the ground and the importance of the match; sometimes the sides were 27 strong, while on special occasions as many as 60 would form a team. In the former case there would be 15 forwards (*innanzi*) in three equal squads, 5 half-backs (*sconciatori*), 4 three-quarter backs (*datori-innanzi*) and 3 goalkeepers (*datori-addietri*). The ball was apparently of the same weight, size and shape as the present-day rugby ball. Each game in the Piazzi was preceded by a pageant consisting of the State and City standard bearers in full uniform accompanied by pages, the Captain of the Halberdiers in full armour at the head of his company, trumpeters, drummers, etc., and finally the players. The whole procession would then encircle the Piazzi twice, after which the players formed a circle in the centre of the ground, holding each other by the hand, so that the presidents could choose the teams and allot each man a place in the field. A trumpet blast was the signal for commencement, and the umpire who, dressed in the colours of both sides, stood in front of the seats of honour, would then throw the ball into the centre of the ground. The rules are rather difficult to follow, but it is interesting to note that 'Two fouls to the disadvantage of the side which scores them are equal to one goal,' and that victory rested with the team which 'won the most goals and scored the fewest fouls'. The players were informed of the end of the game by the discharge of two mortars, and the token of victory was the flag of the vanquished side, which was taken by the winners.

Rugby School, founded about 1567, was one of the direct results of the 'Tuscan Fever' and although the school did not commence to play rugby in a form somewhat similar to the present-day game till 1823, there seems to be little doubt but that 'Il Calcio' was the real origin.

Round About the Ball

E. H. D. SEWELL

*The Gilbert family supplied footballs to Rugby school in the nineteenth
century and the Gilbert name still appears on rugby balls today. James Gilbert
(1885–1967), quoted by E. H. D. Sewell in* Rugger: The Man's Game *(1950),
tells the history of the ball's oval shape. Sewell played cricket for Essex and
rugby for the Harlequins and wrote widely on both sports.*

'IHAVE BEEN UNABLE to trace exactly when the rugby ball first began to assume
its oval shape. Probably some years before 1823. In *Tom Brown's Schooldays*,
in the description of the Bigside game, you will find these words, "The new
ball you may see there quite by itself, in the middle, *pointing* towards the
School goal." There is no doubt therefore of the ball being oval by about 1835,
when this game was supposed to have taken place. By 1851 it had practically
become the same shape as the present time. A ball made for the International
Exhibition, London, in 1851, which we had in our possession, proved this.

Rugby footballs in the early days were made of four pieces of leather
stitched together by hand in the same way as they are today, and were
inflated with pigs' bladders. In this connection an extract from an article
which appeared in a New Zealand paper some years ago is interesting. The
writer of the article speaks of my grandfather. He says he was a bootmaker to
Rugby School, and that he had a great job hunting the countryside for pigs'
bladders with which to inflate the footballs, and that he was locally known as
"the man of the strong lungs" on account of the knack he had of blowing up
the footballs to great resiliency by sheer lung power! Believe me or believe me
not, I have heard it said he used to go as far afield as Birmingham buying up
these pigs' bladders. These unsavoury articles were put into the leather cases
in their 'green' state, the stem of a clay pipe was fastened to the opening of the
bladders and they were then inflated. The balls were then hung up until they
were wanted. You never see a pig's bladder being kicked about now, but when
I was a small boy you very often during the winter used to see a pig's bladder
being kicked about some side street.

The substitution of rubber for the pig's bladder for inflating rugby balls
took place about 1870. Mr Lindon of Rugby first hit upon the idea of making

a bladder of rubber and also invented a pump for inflating it, and so the far from salubrious task of inflating pigs' bladders came to an end.'

⤜❧

Crimson Velvet Caps

JENNY MACRORY

Using 'capped' to indicate selection for your country dates back to the nineteenth century. From Jenny Macrory's wide-ranging history *Running with the Ball: The Birth of Rugby Football* (1991).

THE FIRST FORMAL resolution passed about match dress declared in 1846 that, 'the parties at matches should be distinguished by the colours of their jerseys, the one party wearing white, the other striped jerseys'. This ruling neatly allowed for house colours and emblems to be worn, whilst at the same time providing distinguishing uniforms for contestants in the variously aligned Big Side matches. When the first International match was played a quarter of a century later with no fewer than ten Rugbeians in the England side, the white trousers and jerseys they adopted were derived from the Rugby School dress. Rumour has it that for many years the Captain of England used to ask the permission of the Captain of the School to allow England to use the all-white strip, but this is probably no more than a schoolboy conceit.

The cap is the best known item of football dress to derive from the school. The velvet caps sported in the late 1830s were shaped variously like smoking caps and jockey caps and were worn by those boys sufficiently senior to be allowed to 'play up' in the main body of the match. They were originally brought in as a more practical form of headgear than the top hats which were the ordinary dress and suffered expensively when lost and trampled on the field of play. In the autumn of 1839 Queen Adelaide, the widow of William IV, paid a visit to Rugby School. As a compliment to Her Majesty the boys of School House lined the quadrangle wearing caps in the royal colours of crimson velvet with gold tassels. The Queen later asked to see football played since she had heard it was a pretty spectacle, and the boys immediately obliged regardless of their best dress. The School House played the School, still wearing their royal caps, and so for the first time a team uniform was worn for football. In his autobiography Sir Alexander Arbuthnot recalls that he 'once had the honour of kicking off in a football match before Queen Adelaide'. His football career included introducing the rugby rules to Haileybury, with the exception that 'we abolished running with the ball', and kicking two goals in a match in Madras when a Member of the Council. However he found it 'rather too hot for that sort of fun' and turned his attention instead to founding the Madras Cricket Club in 1846. Here again he was a party to innovative sporting headgear, but this time it did not catch on. 'In my youth,' he said, 'cricketers always played in tall black beaver hats, and I wore a similar top-hat, made of white felt, in India.'

The match watched by Queen Adelaide is confirmed as the first occasion on which uniform team caps were worn by Mr J. G. Holloway in a letter quoted by Sydney Selfe:

> We *did* wear red plush caps as the distinctive mark of the School House players, and we *did* run with the ball *if while on your own side you* could pick it up or catch it in front of goal.

His contemporary, Revd Samuel Sandes, also remembered the crimson velvet caps, but he was the first to point out their true usefulness to players.

> We all wore crimson velvet caps. The custom with the big boys was at the beginning of the football season to send a pair of boots to the shoemaker's in order to have thick soles put on them bevelled at the toes (like a man o' war's bows) so as to cut the shins of the enemy. Often have I seen boys thus lamed sitting on the seats under the elm trees, disabled for further playing, so *to distinguish ourselves in a scrimmage* we wore crimson caps.

The boots Sandes describes were known as 'navvies', and, though they continued to be worn, the evil practice of sharpening the soles, together with other dangers such as metal studs, were abolished by the boys themselves.

> In the match that I refer to, I, being a fast runner, and like a little rat, harder to get at by the dog than a big rat by the dog, was put on the outside by the road. The ball came to me, I caught it up and ran for

dear life to the enemy's goal, where unhurt I touched down. I walked out, kicked up with my heel the sod in the most approved fashion, and placed the ball at the proper angle for Tom Hughes, who kicked our second goal beautifully high. So we won both goals that day, and I felt proud of it, for Arnold and Queen Adelaide were looking on.

Not long after the 1839 match coloured velvet caps were adopted by all the houses, but became a mark of distinction which could only be worn at the invitation of the Head of House. Jerseys were used to distinguish one side from another, while caps denoted players whose performance in lesser games had been good enough to entitle them to 'Follow up' in Big Side Matches. In this way the cap first entered football as a mark of excellence, and in all branches of the sport the pinnacle of a player's career is still to be 'capped' for his country.

A Crucial Misunderstanding

JAMES CORSAN

Early rugby would probably have been totally unrecognisable to today's followers. James Corsan tells how it is highly likely that a mistake was responsible for one of the most characteristic features of modern rugby.
From *For Poulton and England: The Life and Times of an Edwardian Rugby Hero* (2009).

A LTHOUGH WEBB ELLIS did exist – and his name now of course adorns the trophy presented to the Rugby World Cup winning team – the tale of his seminal role in the game is a fabrication all too eagerly adopted by a committee of Old Rugbeians, formed in 1895 as part of a campaign to secure Rugby School's claim to be the sole originator of the handling form of football. A member of the committee, historian Matthew Bloxam, maintained that, in Webb Ellis's time, an attempt to run with the ball towards the goal would have provoked an instant 'hacking over' from the opposition, and possibly worse. Thomas Hughes seemed to concur. He told the committee, apparently without irony, that 'a jury of Rugby boys of the day would almost certainly have found a verdict of justifiable homicide' if a transgressor had been killed in such circumstances. Until well into the second half of the nineteenth century the bulk of the play in a game of rugby football consisted of prolonged scrimmages that progressed slowly, if at all, about the field. In them the majority of participants stood upright – or nearly so – and engaged in pushing and shoving, or alternatively attempting to kick the ball or advance with it wedged between their knees. Only the strongest and keenest sought to wrestle for it or 'pass it on'. On the rare occasions the ball emerged, invariably along the ground, most often it would be kicked or dribbled towards the opposition goal-line. Dribbling is a skill almost lost to rugby today, but until well after the Second World War it was a key weapon in a forward pack's armoury, not least because the shape of the ball then, significantly less pointed than it is today, lent itself splendidly to the practice. A group of two or more forwards bearing down the field, controlling the ball at their feet, was a compelling sight for the opposition. Their best or only method of halting its progress was to launch themselves in front of it in an attempt to gather the ball or somehow hoof it off the park – acts quite likely to result in being on the receiving end of a flying boot or three.

Despite the dominance of the forward battle in the early form of the Rugby School game, at some point before 1840 it became the practice for talented kickers and runners to hang off the scrimmages, ready to make a drop-kick for goal if the ball ever came to them. In due course 'running in', to touch the ball down beyond the goal line, which entitled the scoring team to try for a place kick at goal, became acceptable. In the first written rules of 1845 it was officially permitted, provided it began with a clean catch and that the catcher himself then did the 'running in' *without passing to anyone else*, a qualification whose importance we shall return to shortly.

By the 1860s the popularity of rugby football, on whose behalf Rugbeians, both ex-pupils and masters, were often missionaries, was such that many other schools had either dropped their own version, or else adopted it from scratch. A case in point was Marlborough College, where clergyman George Cotton was headmaster from 1852. One of the unsung heroes of the rise of games in British public school life, in six short years Cotton, formerly a master at Rugby, transformed the direction of the school and made rugby its primary sport. Some fifty-odd years later, one Cecil Hawkins wrote an article in the March 1913 edition of *The Captain*, in which he described in great detail how the game had been played at Marlborough in the 1860s. In it he maintained that rugby's entire history as a passing game was based upon a crucial misunderstanding of both the letter and intention of the original laws of the game as laid down by the RFU. Law 26 – entitled 'Throwing Back' – of *The Laws of the Game of Football as played by the Rugby Football Union* (1871) read as follows:

> It is lawful for any player who has the ball to throw it back towards his own goal, or to pass it back to any player of his own side who is at the time behind him, in accordance with the rules of on-side.

In his piece, having pointed out that the term 'passing' was previously used only in relation to the act of wrestling or handing the ball to a colleague in close proximity, usually in a scrimmage, Hawkins states that this law

> . . . only made it legal to **throw** the ball to a player straight behind you, but it was misunderstood by the new clubs which sprang into existence all over the country, and thereafter throwing the ball to any player who was on side became the vogue and was called 'passing', which it was not . . .

Hawkins's point was that the 1871 Rules never intended that a player with the ball would be allowed to convey it *through the air* to a fellow player, save in one circumstance – that of throwing it back to someone who was following up, directly behind the player with the ball. In support of his contention Hawkins expanded upon the means by which backs at Marlborough in his day were permitted to part with the ball when tackled or held:

> We rarely threw the ball to another player before we were tackled, *as you were only allowed to throw straight back* [author's emphasis]. If a team mate was following you up, you would run straight for the opponent, turn right round as you threw yourself into his arms, and throw the ball back to the man behind you.

The other crucial aspect in the development of the modern game was the reduction of the number of players in a team from twenty to fifteen, a move first taken up by Oxford and Cambridge universities in 1875. The additional pitch space thus released allowed the game to develop from a trial of strength, conducted primarily through a series of prolonged forward scrimmages, into one in which running and passing could flourish. Further impetus was given to the value of running the following year by a new law that, if at the end of the game the number of goals scored by each side was equal, the number of tries would count towards the result. These changes undoubtedly improved the game from the point of view of spectators, as was acknowledged by the previously mentioned Harry 'Jugs' Vassall, the innovative forward of the 1880s, winner of four Oxford blues and five caps for England, who was credited with inventing the (then) three-man three-quarter line:

> We need not pause long to discuss the much-abused shoving matches of the days when twenty a side were played. They have gone never to return, regretted by none, unless perhaps by the modern half-back when he dreams of the glorious chances he would have if the forwards, and especially the wing-players, would only continue to entangle themselves as inextricably as of yore.

Nevertheless there remained a sizeable rump of traditionalists who harked back to the good old days of the game in its original form. In 1896 Thomas Hughes was moved to comment with obvious regret 'Football has got quite beyond me ... it has become too much of a carrying business – football ought to be football, not arm ball ...'

❧

Pride in Their Appearance

PHILIP WARNER

Players' appearance has shifted with the times and fashion. In *The Harlequins* (1991), Philip Warner gives a snapshot of how the earliest players looked.

❧

PLAYERS IN THE 1860s must have looked remarkably different from those of today. Some of the players nowadays have hair which is on the long side, but in the early days of the club short hair would have been conspicuous, not long. No doubt many of their members had beards, and those who did not probably sported moustaches. Amongst their spectators there were no doubt beards which came well down on to the chest. It was the fashion in the nineteenth century to wear a lot of facial hair, often displayed in elaborately trimmed sideboards. The only factor which restrained many a player from grabbing a handful of his opponent's whiskers was the certain knowledge that the inevitable retaliation would include similar treatment of his own.

The grounds on which their early forebears performed were invariably rough fields, whose uneven surface would have been studded with tussocks of grass and occasional shallow holes. Very long grass would be mowed with a scythe. For international matches, the first of which was England v Scotland in 1891, some attempt would have been made to level the field and make it more playable, but most club games took place on fields which were chosen simply because they were less uneven than the others nearby.

Washing facilities were rudimentary, but it must be remembered that these were the days, which lasted well into the present century, when very few houses had proper bathrooms (or inside lavatories). The water supply and sewage system of London in the days when the Harlequins played their early matches were primitive.

Nevertheless, their founder members would have had an impressive appearance (after a wash in cold well water which was so hard that the soap would hardly lather). Elegant, curly-brimmed hats, high collars, colourful cravats, cutaway coats and well-tailored trousers would show that Harlequins took considerable pride in their appearance. Scent was not considered effeminate, but necessary. During the Crusades in the Middle Ages, knights who had to wear their armour for days on end used a lot of scent. It was also popular in the Western Desert in 1942, particularly among tank crews who had no water to spare for washing themselves.

Travel to matches, either home or away, must have presented considerable problems. Although there had been a mania for railway building, the routes were not always convenient for rugger matches and at least some part of the journey would need to be taken in a horse-drawn conveyance, or perhaps on the horse itself. The sight of the Harlequins emerging from a horse-drawn hansom cab must have been a cheering sight.

The telephone was not invented till 1876, and even then it took some time before it became available to the general public. There was therefore no easy way of telling one's opponents not to travel because the ground was flooded or unavailable for other reasons. However, for local messages there were always plenty of errand boys, only too ready to earn a few pence for walking a mile or two.

A Short Guide to Spotting Talent

SUE MOTT

No reviews of rugby basics would be complete without a detailed definition of playing positions. Sue Mott's *A Girl's Guide to Ball Games: What Men Need to Know* (1996) brings a slightly different focus.

'The justification for rugby is getting lashed in decent cities.' (Paul Ackford, former England lock, 1996.)

RUGBY IS A sport that invites men to sellotape their ears to their head and run amok in strict formation. But that is only a dictionary definition. As with all sports, it is the unfettered spirit that counts, especially when served by a barmaid of no mean attribute.

This, of course, implies that rugby union is played by violent alcoholics, somewhat oversized for their age. This is a wicked lie. Some of them, like scrum-halfs, are quite small. Indeed, there is a pleasing logic and democracy about a sport that can cater so well for such dramatically variant shapes and sizes. It is to a prop forward's advantage, for instance, to be shaped like a brick-built coal bunker and share an IQ with a lump of nutty slack. A back, on the other hand can be as cerebral as you like, brighter, lighter, faster, trickier. Swamp Thing meets Tinkerbell.

If one supposed for a moment that female support of rugby union owed anything to the gamut run between no-necked hulks and dainty-footed whizz-kids, it might help to explain the sport's burgeoning popularity and television deals. This may not be remotely true given womankind's traditional high-mindedness. On the other hand, Will Carling's legs did become a major female preoccupation for a while. It would perhaps be foolish to deny that the structure of the player as well as the structure of the game has enormous appeal to those of the female persuasion. In that case, for the uninitiated, a short guide may be in order, all the better to spot talent when you see it.

Hooker – The snarling pit bull terrier of the team whose job it is to hook the ball back through the scrum and intimidate the bone marrow out of every rival back just by being there, glaring and unmuzzled. Built on the squat side, he may be taller lying down, which he often is.

Brian Moore was a hooker. He once challenged a new-found friend to a drinking contest. 'I'll drink this one,' he said, brandishing a bottle of red wine. 'And you drink that one.' Moore did. The friend didn't, sinking to the floor with a third remaining in the bottle. Moore tried to drag him back to consciousness to finish the offending dregs. 'Leave him alone, you animal,' said the distraught wife of the coma victim. 'Haven't you done enough?' That is a hooker.

Props – There are loose-head and tight-head props, which sounds vaguely like a prediction of their physical state after a succession of scrums. These gentlemen are usually conspicuous by their very long arms and almost total lack of neck, which may have been lost on some far-flung field in a previous match.

They are not all insensitive brutes, however. Sean Lynch, the Irish forward, had such a deep-rooted terror of spiders that the day a kind friend and team-mate threw a rubber insect at him on the bus going to a match, he leapt so high in the air in terror his head went through the baggage rack.

Locks – Otherwise known as second row forwards, they are the tall guys of the team, frequently off-duty policemen. I met a Scotsman at Murrayfield who had a theory about this. 'England have a machine that stretches 6ft 5in men until they're 6ft 11in and then they put them in the police force,' he said, whisky in hand. 'They tell them to bash the minorities from Monday morning to Friday night and on Saturdays they bash the Celts.'

Number 8 and the flankers – It is said that brain is now intruding on the brawn, and a trusting nature would seem to be the key asset in this position. Any man willing to shove his head up near the backside of his team-mates in the scrum must have a great deal of faith in their personal habits. But we should not be surprised. The scrum is the physical incarnation of male bonding.

The half-backs – The intelligentsia of the rugby team. The fly-half thinks he is in charge. The scrum-half knows he is in charge. The latter is the easier of the two to spot on the field, by virtue of his pocket size. His job is to retrieve the ball from the scrum and pass it to the fly-half (or stand off) who, like the quarterback in American Football, is regarded as the senior playmaker. This is a sexy position. 'When we won the league championship, all the married guys on the club had to thank their wives for putting up with the stress and strain all season,' said Joe Namath, New York Jets quarterback. 'I had to thank all the single broads in New York.'

Wingers – The speed merchants. Rory Underwood, an RAF jet pilot, was the archetype for England. Then Jonah Lomu of the All Blacks was invented. At that point all comparisons between wingers and whippets became redundant. Now and forever the most apt zoological metaphor would be a charging rhinoceros.

Centres – The sworn enemy of the flankers, these are the cerebral functionaries of the back line. Once again the words 'in theory' require insertion. For although Will Carling, who made his name at centre for England (and in a Chelsea gym, to be fair), passed A levels in English, Geography and Economics, he was rarely accused of being a dry academic.

Full-back – In theory, the goalkeeper, protected from the mêlée by his withdrawn position. In fact, the man most likely to be trampled. How does one qualify for the post? 'The reason I played full-back was because I wore glasses and couldn't see,' said a former schoolboy prodigy. 'If you can't see what's steaming towards you, you can't be afraid.' But you can learn. He's in banking now.

Of such characters the wonderful game is comprised. But as any discussion with a rugby aficionado will prove, the main attraction of the sport is not the tactics but The Tour. Going away, *en masse* and insensible, is what it's all about. In quaint bygone days, when women knew their place (and it wasn't in the second row), the men had the frivolity of the tour to themselves. No more. Women have learned to join in.

. . . Whether rugby women are as bad, or indeed worse, for drink as their male counterparts is one of those points which will never be resolved. In masculine minds, there is no contest: 'If the girls get as drunk as the men, it doesn't work,' said a man on a train bound for Murrayfield. 'They let themselves down a bit. I think we've got a higher standard of drunkenness.'

The women don't see it as a contest either. 'I think we're fairly horrific,' said Clare, Ireland supporter and nurse. 'But men are worse because they get so trashed they don't make any sense. We never sink quite to the same depths when we're pissed.'

Either way those depths and depravations are an inexpungible part of rugby's innocent attraction and there are many ways a drink-fuelled rugby sort can enjoy him/herself while away from the domestic rein.

Furniture Removal – On the 1974 British Lions tour to South Africa, the great Willie John McBride had graduated from one of the lads to elder statesman of the team. He looked on, but rarely joined in. On one particular night, the manager of the team hotel was becoming rather concerned for the safety of his fixtures and fittings in the hands of thirty hairy, hulking and, by now, rather boisterous players. 'I have to tell you,' said the hotel manager anxiously, 'that I shall be forced to call the local police if this carries on.' McBride looked at the manager and puffed gently on his pipe. 'Tell me this,' he said finally. 'Will there be many policemen?'

Exaggerated Behaviour – Moss Keane, the monster lock from Kerry, gained forty-one caps for Ireland and one ardent admirer from Australia the day he engaged her in idle conversation. ''Scuse me, are you the Moss?' enquired a petite, blonde Aussie girl of the second rower. He agreed to the charge. 'You know,' she said, 'you are one hell of big man.' He assented again. With her eyes barely reaching his belt buckle, she further enquired: 'Are you all in proportion?' He was forced to admit he was not. The light died in her eyes, only to be rekindled when he said: 'If I was in proportion I'd be 9ft 10in.'

∽

2

INVOCATIONS

Ka Mate Haka

ATTRIBUTED TO CHIEF TE RAUPARAHA, *c.*1820

The best known of the many hakas is probably the Ka Mate,
first performed by the All Blacks in 1905.

❧

Leader:	Ringa pakia!	Slap the hands against your thighs!
	Uma tiraha!	Puff out your chest!
	Turi whatia!	Bend your knees!
	Hope whai ake!	Then the hips!
	Waewae takahia kia kino!	Stamp your feet as hard as you can!

Leader:	Ka mate! Ka mate!	Death is at hand! I am going to die!

Team:	Ka ora! Ka ora!	No, you will live, you will live!

Leader:	Ka mate! Ka mate!	It is death, I am going to die!

Team:	Ka ora! Ka ora!	You will live, you will live!

All:	Tenei te tangata puhuruhuru	This is the strong man
	Nana nei tiki mai	Who caused the sun to shine
	whakawhiti te ra	again for me
	A upane! Ka upane!	A step upward! Another step upward!
	A upane kaupane!	Up to the top!
	Whiti te ra!	The sun shines!
	Hi!	Rise!

The Art of Haka

PHIL SHIRLEY

The historical background and cultural significance of the haka is
explained in an extract from *Blood and Thunder: The Unofficial Biography of
Jonah Lomu* (1999).

～❧

T HE ALL BLACKS have always excelled in the art of haka, which is the
generic term for Maori dance. Henare Teowai of Ngati Porou, an
acknowledged master of the art of haka, was asked on his death-bed, 'What
is the art of performing haka?' He replied: '*Kia korero te katoa o te tinana*', 'The
whole body should speak.'

...The haka is a composition played by many instruments. Hands, feet, legs,
body, voice, tongue and eyes all play their part in blending together to convey
in their fullness the challenge, welcome, exultation, defiance or contempt of
the words. Lomu, like most All Blacks, has spent hours getting it right. It is
disciplined, yet emotional. More than any other aspect of Maori culture, this
complex dance is an expression of the passion, vigour and identity of the race.
It is, at its best, truly, a message of the soul expressed by words and posture.
There are several styles of haka. Ka Mate was originally of the *ngeri* style,
which is a short, free-form haka where the performers interpret as they feel
fit. It is also performed without weapons, and is not therefore a war-dance as
is generally supposed. The *peruperu* is a style of haka for true war-dance. It
involves weapons and is characterised by a high jump with legs folded under
at the end. Observers of the All Blacks will note that they perform this same
jump, which is a point of irritation among haka purists. In fact the All Black
rendition of Ka Mate may have undergone quite a few changes along the way
to make it more impressive.

A few years ago, around 1995 or 1996, the All Blacks' famous haka ruffled
the feathers of sections of the very Maori community from where it originated.
The then New Zealand Maori rugby coach Matt Te Pou said the Ka Mate
version of the haka used by the All Blacks was identified with the nineteenth-
century warrior chief Te Rauparaha, who slaughtered South Island Maoris
during several forays south. 'He decimated the local Maori down there,' Te
Pou said. The haka performance itself, which overseas is more well known than

the New Zealand national anthem, was too important to dispense with so it nevertheless remained.

As far as rugby is concerned the first haka in an overseas representative match was performed by the New Zealand Native Team which toured the UK in 1888–9. It isn't clear whether or not it was Ka Mate which they performed, but it is probable. At many venues they went to some trouble to entertain, bringing out mats and other items onto the field to complement the performance. In fact this team was not entirely composed of Maori, as many assume. The tour was not officially sanctioned, and cost each player the large sum of £250 passage. This made it impossible to find the required number of Maori, and at least two 'dark-skinned' *pakeha* (i.e. white New Zealanders) were included. The first use of the haka by the All Blacks was by the 'Originals' in 1905 on the first overseas tour by a full-scale New Zealand representative side. It was also on this tour that the name 'All Blacks' was first used. The two most distinctive features of the New Zealand team were thus instigated right from the very beginning. The haka became a permanent fixture for the All Blacks from then on.

One famous anecdote is told regarding the 1924 New Zealand team, which became known as the famous 'Invincibles', due to their winning every match on tour. This team had as their most famous son a young Maori boy called George Nepia. He it was who led the All Black haka, Ka Mate, in the first match against Devon on 13 September 1924. The haka was enthusiastically received by the crowd of 18,000, who then watched the All Blacks win 11–0, but a 'prominent university sportsman' who attended was moved to write a letter which appeared in the next day's paper. In it he asserted: 'Cat-calls were quite uncalled-for' and added: 'South Africans do not open their games with Zulu cries!' Obviously, this gentleman had never visited either country.

The words of Ka Mate do not have direct relevance to rugby and in the case of the All Blacks the 'loose' translation of the haka challenge is:

We are the All Blacks, of the New Zealand people. Here we are to face you. We will do you the honour of playing to the limits that our hearts and sinews impose upon us. We will be very hard to beat.

❧

A Show of Respect

BRIAN O'DRISCOLL

O'Driscoll was captain of the 2005 British and Irish Lions in New Zealand.
In *A Year in the Centre* (2005), he describes how he went to great lengths to
avoid offending New Zealand sensibilities during the performance of the haka
in the first Test.

❧

FROM THE VERY start of the tour we had discussed, at some length, how to
accept the haka before the Test, because for the All Blacks that's clearly
where the game begins. Also, you can encounter a haka at almost any time
before or after a game in New Zealand. We have bent over backwards to
do everything by the book on this tour and not to upset any Maori or New
Zealand sensibilities. This is their country, we are visitors and we are trying to
do the right thing. So when we discussed how to accept the haka at the first
Test, Clive [Woodward] mentioned a number of emails he had received on the
subject, including one from a Maori elder which detailed exactly how it should
be done with the maximum of respect. These instructions were consistent with
advice we received from the Maori welcoming party all those weeks ago in
Rotorua.

We followed his plan to the letter. I, as the warrior chief, stepped forward
directly opposite their chief – Tana Umaga – to accept the challenge,
accompanied, as best practice dictates, by our youngest warrior, Dwayne Peel.
The rest of the team fanned out across the pitch and remained as motionless
as Easter Island statues. It was an exhilarating moment.

As protocol demands, I tried to maintain eye contact with Tana and remain
still, even though it was freezing cold and I could feel muscles tightening up,
especially my hamstring, which I always like to keep warm in the immediate
build-up to the game. I normally keep my tracksuit bottoms on during the
anthems back home and sometimes have the masseur run on and work on my
hamstring there and then. But we decided to bin that to avoid any possible
misinterpretation.

Tana always seems to get pretty worked up when he leads the haka – it's
an incredible advantage for the All Blacks to perform it while their opponents
stand there subservient and powerless – but it's part of the tradition and a

Lions tour is about maintaining tradition. But this time he seemed to be particularly animated and hyped up.

When the haka was finished it was time to formally accept the challenge. As the Maori elder in the email had instructed, I leaned forward while still maintaining eye contact, clutched a piece of grass from the pitch and threw it to the wind. It went properly, thank God. Tana, though, was still looking extremely agitated.

I've subsequently been told that some of the All Blacks and spectators thought we had insulted them by the manner in which we received the haka. That is just too incredible for words. We had done our homework thoroughly and made every effort to ensure we behaved in textbook fashion, and now I have to put up with this crap. The truth is that at Christchurch on Saturday night we understood and respected the haka a little bit better than some of the All Blacks and many of their camp followers and media who have been whinging today. What more do they want from us?

They have to show us respect as well. If it's a problem with us smiling or twitching at the wrong time – as has been suggested – there is a very simple solution. We can do away with the haka. Then we can't possibly offend anybody and we can all start on a level playing field.

A Prayer

J. J. STEWART

This 'prayer' was written by J. J. Stewart, coach of the Wanganui-King Country side and later of the All Blacks from 1973 to 1976, before the combined side played the British and Irish Lions in 1971.

Amen I say unto you whosoever shall pass the ball under conditions more
    advantageous to the opposition than his own team will be cast aside.
Verily let it always be that our defence will be desperate and those who
    set up second phase play behind the forwards shall feel the wrath of
    the Almighty.

May we always remember to concentrate not on winning but on not losing.

It will come to pass that the ball shall be kept ahead of the forwards, and in so doing may we always remember it can be done by passing or kicking, and kicking is simple, and as we consider these and other faults let us be mindful that he who adopts the involved dog position in the rucks shall be smote with a bucketful of water.

From these sins and the national selectors may the Lord protect us.

Dominus Tackle, Dominus Tackle, Dominus Tackle.

Amen.

3

FOR THE LOVE OF IT

Mid-Life Crisis

STEPHEN GAUGE

When you take up rugby as an adult, the question 'Are you a forward or a back?' is not necessarily easy to answer. From *My Life as a Hooker: When a Middle-Aged Bloke Discovered Rugby* (2012).

❧

WHEN YOU TAKE up a team sport like rugby as an adult, even if you have absolutely no idea what you are doing, no one gives you a hard time. People are just pathetically grateful that you have turned up. They are nice to you because you have made up the numbers so that they can have a proper game. If you add to that a willingness to play in the front row, they can have contested scrums and you will have made some friends for life.

Rugby seemed to be a great place to deal with my own personal midlife crisis. I was in a relatively senior job in a large chamber of commerce and government-funded business support operation. Having spent the earlier part of my career in a more metrosexual media and political environment, I was now surrounded by some very blokey blokes; they were all either go-getting entrepreneurial types, or failed businessmen who had become business advisers. Most seemed to spend their days talking about sport and cars. If I was going to get on with this crowd, as the saying goes, I needed to 'man up'.

I had also recently acquired contact lenses after a lifetime in glasses in a bout of midlife vanity. It could have been worse: others of my generation were bleaching their hair, getting inappropriate piercings and wearing leather trousers. Contact lenses paved the way to contact sports.

So when I found my way to Warlingham Rugby Club, I was delighted to discover a home for a group of men, all enjoying their own particular mid-, early- or later-life crises and having a good time into the bargain. Here, by a Surrey playing field in the late summer, I found my way to the changing rooms and pulled on my newly purchased boots.

Warlingham is like many rugby clubs in the UK. There is a nice enough clubhouse with a huge function room, a cosy bar and some basic, bare-brick changing rooms. It prides itself on being one of the few clubs with a huge traditional communal bath. It has five pitches and shares the premises with a netball team and a cricket club. Every now and again someone will apply for some lottery money, send out an appeal or send off an insurance claim and a few improvements or repairs will be done by someone's mate.

There is a floodlit training pitch and on a Tuesday and Thursday evening throughout the autumn, winter and spring, men of various shapes and sizes turn up for training.

It's only when you look at the car park on a training night that you realise the wide range of people that get involved. One of the joys of amateur club rugby is the diversity of the sorts of people who play. From city boys who turn up in suits and smart cars, to builders and landscape gardeners who turn up in battered Ford Transit vans, once everyone is changed and on the pitch your background is almost irrelevant. Traditional British social divisions are replaced by a far more sinister and uncrossable barrier, rugby's very own apartheid: the distinction between forwards and backs.

That was the first tricky decision I had to make at my first training session. After a bit of running around to warm up we were told to divide up into forwards and backs. Which was I? I had absolutely no idea, and no time to decide. As far as I could tell, from watching the odd international on the TV, the forwards seemed to have to do a lot of fairly technical stuff: scrums, line-outs, rucks, mauls, ear-biting, eye-gouging etc. These were dark acts of which I knew nothing. The backs seemed to have a fairly straightforward job of standing in a line, throwing the ball to each other and running a bit. How hard could that be? I decided to be a back.

The coach for that evening was a nice bloke called Neil Farmer, a ponytailed schoolteacher (pottery, I guessed), tall and thin with a good line in sarcasm. He took one look at me as I jogged off to join the backs and, with his eyebrows making a bid for freedom off the top of his head, said, 'Are you sure?'

I'm not a hugely tall person and the modest belly that I carry around with me for comfort and protection is ever so slightly out of proportion with my height. The coach, as might anyone else, looked at me and saw an overweight hobbit who ought to be in the front row, if anywhere at all.

However, I stuck with the backs for the first session. A seventeen-year-old with enormous patience told me where to stand, when to run and what to do if I caught the ball. We ran around a bit and passed the ball to each other. In the words of Aleksandr the Meerkat, 'Simples.'

One of the things that have impressed me about club rugby is that I can't think of many other situations where a middle-aged fat bloke can interact socially with hoody-wearing teenagers. Probably the only other time it happens is when you're being mugged. Talking to teenagers is normally unbearably painful. Add a rugby ball into the equation, however, and suddenly it seems to work. It turns out that they can actually be quite pleasant. The young man who looked after me at my first session on the playing fields of Warlingham Rugby Club did a great job and I've never looked back.

I did quickly realise, however, that I was never going to be a back. There really was an awful lot of running around involved. An independent assessment of my physique by the third-team captain, Mark O'Connor, suggested that I was the perfect stature to become a hooker. That's the chap in the middle of the front row of the scrum who has the job of hooking back the ball with his foot, so that it pops out of the back of the scrum into the grateful hands of the scrum-half.

I was delighted that my potential had been spotted so early – that someone had singled me out for this important and highly technical position. Little did I realise that Mark O'Connor, like every other club captain in every other club, would have the unenviable job of finding at least three people, week in week out, prepared to risk their necks in the middle of the scrum. Surrey physiotherapists were rubbing their cash registers with glee as another poor misguided fool volunteered for the front row.

As it turned out, hooking was a great job for me as someone completely new to the game who didn't really know what was going on elsewhere on the pitch. I had two clear tasks and both of them were part of restarting the game. I had to throw the ball in at the line-out and hook the ball back in the scrum. The rest of the game was far too chaotic and complicated for me at that stage, and much of it still is.

As a hooker, I wasn't going to have too many decisions to make about where to go and what to do. I could generally run around, keeping close enough to the play to look as if I was involved, whilst remaining just far enough away to avoid getting hurt. Then when the game stopped the referee would either call for a scrum or a line-out and then I had one or other of my two jobs to do.

So my position was sorted. I was beginning to feel ready for a proper game.

A Game for Spartans

W. ROWE HARDING

The atmosphere of village rugby in Wales during the 1920s forms the centre of this evocative extract from *Rugby Reminiscences and Opinions* (1929). Harding played seventeen times for Wales in the 1920s.

THE STRENGTH OF Welsh rugby lies in the villages rather than in the big towns. Association football has challenged the sway of rugby in Swansea and Cardiff, where it once reigned as absolute monarch, but in the village rugby is still the game, although the increased transport facilities and new-fangled amusements like the 'talkies' are making it hard for the village clubs to retain the support necessary to run the clubs and pay the costs of charabanc hire and rents. I had a year's experience of village rugby before I went to Swansea, and very good fun it was. It is a game for Spartans, because dressing accommodation is seldom other than primitive. Few clubs can afford a pavilion, and so the headquarters are at the village 'pub', and both teams usually change together in the club room, and perform their after-the-match ablutions in tin baths, brought in for the purpose. No one is ever certain when the game will start, because the visiting team for a variety of reasons may be late. The charabanc may have broken down; the driver may have lost his way. They may have had to wait for a miner member of the side who has been 'working on'. It is no unusual sight in a village match to see a coal-black visage among the white faces of the other players, because some of the players come straight from the pithead to the football field. I have often been amazed at the stamina and endurance of these Welsh miners and steel-workers. After a hard day's work before a blazing furnace, or in a two-foot seam, ordinary men would feel like a rest, but your village rugby player thinks nothing of ending up a strenuous day's work with a game of rugby, and very hard and dour rugby at that. I have known many instances where miners who have worked all Friday night and on Saturday morning have come down to Swansea and played hard rugby in the afternoon, or have rushed home after a match and gone on to work at six o'clock in the evening. I have known many, too, who have sacrificed a 'double shift' at the week-end to play for Swansea, or even for a village club in an important match on Saturday afternoon.

There is nothing quite like a 'Derby' match between two neighbouring Welsh clubs. The mild rivalry which exists between Blackheath and the Harlequins is but a pale shadow of the intense hatred which is worked up between two near neighbours in Wales when they meet in their annual trial of strength and skill. The supporters of the visiting team invade the enemy territory hours before the start, pour into their strongholds and stay there until they are turned out by the landlord. Betting is not unusual on these occasions, nor are fights unknown. The match is fought out in an electric and noisy atmosphere, and fought out sometimes in the literal interpretation of the term. After the game the victors celebrate their victory, and the vanquished drown their sorrows, and so it is all the same in the end. I hasten to add that all Welsh matches are not played in that spirit, and this seems the appropriate place to discuss the question of rough play.

Personally I resent the accusations of foul play which are often recklessly made against Welsh rugby as though it was peculiar to Wales. Rough rugby is often played in England, and I have played in such matches in the West Country and in college cup matches at Cambridge. The difference between rough rugby in England and rough rugby in Wales is largely a matter of accent. An old Cambridge Blue once made the remark that rugby is essentially a game for gentlemen, and no truer remark was ever made. At rugby the better side must necessarily win only when both sides play according to the letter and spirit of the rules and of the game. The word 'gentleman', however, does not connote membership of any social class, and I have known Varsity players who were not gentlemen, and miners who were. The ethics of fair play in rugby are really much more complicated than some spectators realise. It is the claim of rugby players that, after all, the game is their game, and does not belong to the spectators. They can come and watch if they like, but it is a matter of indifference to the players whether they do or not. I have observed that complaints of rough play often emanate from the spectators, when the players themselves are perfectly satisfied with the game. Hacking and fisticuffs revolt the sensitive spectator, and speaking as a somewhat frail wing three-quarter, I must say I never cared for that kind of thing myself, but it is well recognised among rugby forwards that in some circumstances hacking is permissible, and within the spirit of the game. I never saw a Scottish forward draw back his foot during a dribble because an opponent was trying to pick up the ball, nor have I often seen a forward jump over a man who was wilfully lying on the ball. It is an accepted maxim among forwards that a man who deliberately lies on the ball deserves to be kicked, and he is kicked. Gentlemen, however, kick a man with the instep, not the toe of the boot, and kick the offender on that part of his anatomy which is designed by nature for chastisement. In an ordinary game of rugby fisticuffs cannot be justified on any grounds whatever; fighting is one game, and rugby another, and although we players may profess to ignore the spectator, we must not forget that without him our trips to Ireland, to France and to the Colonies would be quite impossible. He deserves consideration, and for his sake forwards should not offend his susceptibilities by matching their punching power with that of their opponents in the line-out. Still, I have met some good fellows in rugby who were not above striking a blow in retaliation, and it is a well-known test of good fellowship among forwards that a man can take a knock as well as give one.

I know two international forwards, one English, the other Irish, who are great friends, but who wage a perpetual vendetta on the rugby field, and it is said that in one international match they were both in danger of being sent off for fighting until the referee observed the good-humoured grins on their faces. Still, even good-humoured scrapping is not to be encouraged on the rugby field, because a fighting rugby forward is of no more use than a fighting greyhound.

∾

High on Oysters and Pouilly-Fumé

RICHARD BEARD

Novelist Richard Beard moves from mid-Argyll to Paris
'prepared for changes'. From *Muddied Oafs: The Last Days of Rugger* (2003).

∾

THE RUGBY IN Paris was often full of charm, the French quickness of thought with the ball in hand a sporting vision of wit, and their liberated approach to the game is reflected in the language. The fly-half is the *ouvreur*, who opens the game, in contrast to the dour English equivalent who closes it down with a fifty-metre punt. In France, the patterns of a match have none of the rigidity of the British version, and it's a commonplace that the game begins on the wing. Defences change rapidly from solid to liquid. Stone is suddenly paper, and cut to pieces. To ribbons.

This theatrical tradition of flair and disguise can be captivating, and in 2002 I was full of the joys of French rugby as I sat swaying on the Métro on the way to training, high on a dozen oysters and a litre of Pouilly-Fumé. It may have been the wine, but I was feeling good about my chances of survival. The cut eye from Glasgow was now a decent buttery black, but nicely fringed with reddish brown, a real shiner, making me look less like me and more like a hard case from the SCUF's [Sporting Club Universitaire de France] mercenary past. On the negative side, on the sober side, I still couldn't lift my arms above my shoulders.

I was prepared for changes. A club like the SCUF based in a big city like Paris has a different character and different problems from a rural, community-based club like mid-Argyll. For a start, the SCUF play their matches at the Stade Georges Carpentier, but they don't own it. And during the week they have to find other open spaces where they can train, a growing problem for an amateur club in an era when nothing is free or even cheap, especially open spaces in the centre of capital cities. It's also in the nature of a city club to have a high turnover of players, making it unlikely there'd be many people I recognised. It was nearly ten years since I'd last trained there, after all.

Unlike mid-Argyll, the SCUF have no problem with numbers. There were at least fifty people out on the gravelly floodlit surface, though I stopped counting at twenty-nine or so, because we were all running round and round in circles and I was getting dizzy.

I knew there'd be trouble as soon as I saw the coaches. There were two of them, both small and bald in ironed rugby shirts, and I recognised the littler of the two from '93. Soubras had sometimes let him wet the sponges. Both of them had clipboards *and* whistles *and* stopwatches. And also a tape-measure. The senior coach, who was marginally taller, had a neatly trimmed tonsure at the back of his head, and wore long shorts over his immaculate track-suit trousers, which in turn were primly tucked into his pulled-up socks. He unfolded a camping stool on which to sit and talk (and talk and talk), while the players sat on the ground around him. We then passed the ball meaninglessly in lines of four. One direction, stop, then the other. Repeat.

Later, we ran round in a circle roughly the size of the pitch, non-stop for thirty minutes, while the coach measured the white lines with the tape-measure. This was so that he'd know how far we'd run. He could then write this down on his clipboard.

Jean-Claude Soubras used to have us one-to-one wrestling while insulting our mothers.

At the end of training, I approached Monsieur Rausch, as the senior coach was called, and of course complimented him fulsomely on what a very fine job he appeared to be doing. I then asked him politely if by any chance I might be able to get a game on the Sunday, which is always match-day in France.

Monsieur Rausch looked at me sternly, and told me that SCUF were off for a weekend's squad fitness session and pre-season practice match at Le Touquet-Paris-Plage, not far from Calais.

'Sounds like fun. What are my chances of a game?'

He frowned and referred to a small booklet, of which he had several, and not all of them small. He then said he doubted very much whether I'd be able to play, for complex reasons of insurance.

'How complex?'

'I'll need to refer to the Federation regulations.'

'Fine,' I said and drifted off to the showers. People in rugby were increasingly saying such things, but I was sure that after another session on Thursday it would all seem easier. In fact, only the week before Brocken had been telling me about the time he and big Davy had come over, eight or nine years ago, and Peter Mackinnon had drafted them into an over-thirty-fives match on a Sunday morning. One of the SCUF props had then whistled the Scots round the Champs Elysées and the Eiffel Tower, wherever they wanted to go.

That's what rugby was all about, and that night I went to sleep dreaming of the beautiful game, particularly in France, where college professors publish books with titles like *Dans le Temple du Dieu Rugby*. To the French, of course, that deceptive, infuriating ball, which never bounces in the expected direction, just has to be a woman. She's unreliable, desirable, valuable, dangerous. She prefers a strong man with strong arms who knows how to hold her tight. But if he doesn't, if he takes her for granted, she'll soon move on to another ... *putain*!

The French are essential to the global health of rugby union. They constantly bring fresh and surprising perspectives to the game, saving it from a slow death as an arcane celebration between former British colonies. They can also beat the All Blacks. Abdelatif Benazzi, for example, the immovable French forward with sixty-five caps (and twelve for Morocco), has personally beaten New Zealand the same number of times as the four home nations put together. I have a theory about this. The French can't be intimidated by sledging, by those gritty All Black vowel sounds which reminds the Brits of generations of All

Black invincibles. The French don't understand a word. They just get on with it and win, and remain the best living proof that the game can transcend its Empire origins – we owe all our ambitions to them.

. . . Along with its charm, the French game can also be brutal, and French rugby has had to steal from English to accommodate the notion of *le fair play*. There is no equivalent word in the French vocabulary, and as the SCUF's best player, Trevor Wright was often knocked to bits. As well as being the finest broken-play runner ever to wait for me behind the posts, where he'd lob the ball to gift me a score, he was also the first player I saw injected in the dressing room before a match. The needle went into the side of his knee, right behind the knee-cap. He was the club's investment. It was a crucial play-off game. *Bah voilà*.

However, not all the drugs in French rugby are in the trainer's bag (more commonly known as *la pharmacie*). In French-speaking countries, the game of rugby is cool. Cool in the rock-star sense. At a time when rugby and rugger were two of the most unfashionable words in the English language, in France *le rugby* was darkly seductive, a virile sport associated with manly combat, love of good food, and festivals (the riotous *bandas* of the south-west). The *Midi-Olympique* used to report on rugby in the winter and bull-fighting in the summer, *le rugbyman* as a winter matador, El Cordobes with the ears of the bull held aloft in his outstretched hands. He is *rugbyman*, a cartoon-book super-hero, and the clubs are full of *rugbymen*, entire graphic novels of them.

The French rugby player carries none of the rugger-bugger baggage which weighs so heavily, often with good reason, on the rounded shoulders of the English. He is an upright and heroic participant in a noble and dangerous enterprise which requires great courage and sacrifice of the self, and quite commonly also long hair and soft drugs and a two-tone VW camper van.

In Paris, rugby provided all the experiences I'd fantasised as a dividend of published fiction; long lunches in restaurants, cigarettes, late nights in dives, *pastis*, heated conversations about the essence of existence, and passing relationships with a huge range of interesting people, including François the front-row forward who tended the Shakespeare garden in the Bois du Boulogne. In Paris, even the ugly municipal gardeners have a series of breathtaking foreign girlfriends, the pick of the *jeune filles au pairs* who spend so much time wheeling rich French babies around public parks. As a mark of tender affection, François would sew his current girlfriend's national flag on the back of his denim work jacket.

Adventures in the Shin Trade

FRANK KEATING

One of the finest sports writers of his era recalls his early journalistic
career and his ambitions to play for Gloucester in the mid-1950s.
From *Up and Under* (1983).

❧

FROM THE *STROUD News* and *Hereford Times*, both weeklies, I had graduated,
briefly, to the big time – an evening paper. Though I was then a sub-editor
on general news – Women's Institute expert, flower shows a speciality – we
were expected to help put the Saturday sports 'Pink 'Un' to bed. County rugger
Saturdays were very special editions. On those afternoons the *Gloucester Citizen*
employed extra boys to race the 'running' paragraphs from the Kingsholm
press box; a dash down Dean's Walk, a hare up Hare Lane with a breathless
skid into the sports editor's tray in St John's Lane. The world was waiting. And
'the world' then meant the *Citizen*'s sister 'Pinks', at Cheltenham and Bristol.
Is the *Citizen* still the only Pink in Britain invariably to lead its front page
with rugby? 'Where do you want Cinderford v. Coney Hill to go?' I would ask
the sports editor, furiously attacking a scrap of ill-typed paper with my biro.
'*Front!*' he would scream. And later, 'What page Manchester United v Spurs,
sir?' 'Page six,' he would mumble dismissively.

By the tag-end of the fifties I was working on that same southerly sister, the
Bristol Evening World. It was like yesterday that I was sweating on the runner
of the 1959 final as the paragraph came into the office from the Memorial
Ground. We were leading the match until near the end and I had even written
the headline, 'GLOSHIRE DO IT!' – then the last flash came through telling of
Warwickshire's final try and the nail being hammered in by George Cole
of the boot. That was the start of Warwickshire's seven titles in eight years.
Nobody has bettered that mighty spasm. But 'Glorse' have come close.

Oddly enough, Gloucestershire won their first final against Yorkshire – in
1910. In my day, you could still meet old men in pubs who would reverently
place their pint pot on a table, lower their eyes, and recite the team that day:
'Johnson, Hudson, Spoors, Neale, Eberle' (pause for a sip, then even more
reverence), 'Dai Gent and Jimmy Stephens'. (Another swig before the pack
would come out in an eightsome rush): 'Johns, Berry, Uzzell, 'Olford and

'Ollands, Gardner, Wright 'n Bowkett.' Gloucester won that game 23–0 and contemporary reports began, 'It was a beautiful spring day and the ground was in tip-top condition . . .'

Gloucestershire's tradition – in which they exult, sometimes boringly – has been of rough, tough forwards, fist-happy thickoes from the Forest of Dean or from the bleak midwinter villages on the hills above the Severn plain. Yet I was privileged to be in on John Blake's running team at Bristol in the fifties and sixties. What a man! He revolutionised the game long before new rules could. As a fly-half he had to run – because he could not kick. Week after week he inspired his mates to run with him through every tackler as though all fifteen of them were demented electronic pinballs. Blake's Bristol XV scored try upon glorious try. An England selector once came down to pick him for Twickenham but sadly pronounced – 'Brilliant he is, but how can a man play for England if he cannot kick?'

Gloucestershire rugby more than most owes its strength and historical eminence to the small clubs from which it feeds so voraciously. Time without number have I scanned the names of the latest county selection and despairingly read the parenthesis 'Gloucester' or 'Bristol'. We exiles want to know where a new lad learned his game – in Longlevens, Lydney or Cheltenham, in Stroud or Clifton or Cirencester, or Cainscross or the Gordon League, or Painswick, or Pates or St Pauls . . . But, simply, if you want to play for the county you have got to join Bristol or Gloucester.

In their centenary brochure a few years back the Stroud club reflected: 'If there is a weakness in Gloucestershire rugby it lies in the fact that in the last two or three seasons Bristol and Gloucester, because of their successes on the field of play, have attracted to their ranks more good players than they need. A place on the touchline as a travelling reserve or a run around in the "United" is no training ground for the modern game. This is not knocking at our old friends, Bristol and Gloucester. It is vital to the game in the county that they should be strong. It is equally vital that Stroud, Lydney, Cheltenham and Clifton should be strong.'

I was once 'attracted' to Gloucester. Having brought me up midway between the shrine at Kingsholm and one of its attendant altars, at Fromehall in Stroud, my father went and did a daft thing: he sent me away to school – and not only that, but a school in the dreaded Home Counties. A rugger establishment, sure. But not at all the same thing as a Gloucestershire rugger school.

So a fancypants scrum-half came back to Gloucester in the middling 1950s. My first-hand experience – or rather *second*, for I was surely concussed most of the time – did not last very long. I probably had the shortest 'career' in big-time sport since another local lad, Sam Cook, the Tetbury plumber and left-handed bowler, played his one single Test match for England – nought for plenty against South Africa in 1947.

Anyway, armed with a letter and encouragement from our rugby master at school to continue my rugby career, I turned up for late-summer training trials at Kingsholm. Yes, I thought, aim for the top, bypass Stroud and Cainscross. I turned up in Persilled shorts and gleaming new Cotton-Oxfords. That was my first mistake. I saw a diabolic gleam in the eye of Peter Ford as I was introduced in the locker room – he was a destroyer of half-backs for England as well as for Gloucestershire. My second mistake was to allow myself to be picked on the opposite side to Peter in the muck-around touch rugby game that followed the training session. *Touch* rugby! The first time I touched the ball Mr Ford, my marker, compressed me to the earth like a flea under a copper's foot. I was scraped up, rolled to the touchline and left for dead.

Years later, browsingly reviewing the rugby autobiography of one of Ford's apprentices around that time, that amiable hard nut with the soft centre, Mike Burton, I found myself breaking into a shiver. This is what Burton wrote about a typical Gloucester pre-match team talk: 'Mickey Booth, who was captain, would pass among us uttering gruff, mumbling noises. When we were ready, Booth would address the assembly. "Just give me the ball," he would say. "I want you donkeys to give me the ball and I'll do the rest. Anything to say, Peter?" He always called on the experienced Ford. The man himself stood up, glistening and toothless. "Just good old-fashioned stuff. Get in and 'it 'em hard" – one of the precepts of the Gloucester legend. Ford was ruthless, and under the old rules which allowed flankers to creep round scrums he made the lives of many scrum-halves a misery.'

Anyway, that touch rugby night at Kingsholm saw me helped home by Russell Hillier, a Stroudite who *could* stand the heat and, indeed, went on to play for the county. Next morning I had to be driven to Dr Kinsella's surgery in Stonehouse. He laughed, too, and said I had all the symptoms of shellshock. Gloucester never sent me another postcard – and when I telephoned them to ask when I could come and collect my boots a man suggested that if I was still keen on having an occasional game 'then I should give Stroud Nomads a ring'. So I never did get to hear Peter Ford's longest speech – before a county semi-final: 'If it's dark and moves kick it; it might be the ball. If it's dark and still just stand on it. If it squeals, say "Sorry" in earshot of the ref.'

What a player Ford was! Coincidentally, his one international season for England was in 1964 in an untechnical era of fast and loose, destructive flankers – and he packed down alongside Mike Davis and Budge Rogers, [later] respectively England's coach and chairman of selectors. Blimey, what sort of England coach would Peter Ford have made! His combative philosophies would have made establishments quake.

Higgledy-piggledy, Gloucester names trip off the tongue as I write . . . Hook and Hall and Hudson and Hastings and Hopson and Haines; Terrington and Ibbotson, Jones and Nicholls; Watkins and Smith and Fowke; Booth and Blakeway and Boughton and Burton and Bayliss and Brinn and Boyle and Butler . . . but I suppose the most shining light in the legend, top of the roll of honour, remains Tom Voyce, who played for England through the 1920s. The All Blacks came over in 1925, bone-hard, closed-knuckled, mean-eyed and nasty. Certainly they looked to get their retaliation in first – and certainly the opening quarter-hour of the Twickenham international was mind-boggling in its explosive dirtiness. Then Voyce – already with a cut eye and lip – turned to Wavell Wakefield, his battered captain, and said with a grin through the gore, 'Up with your sleeves, my old skip. By golly, it's real good fun, isn't it? I didn't know these buggers went in as hard as this.' I met Tom Voyce once, at a 'do' in a hotel near Amberley. He was an old man, but spry. I asked him if that story was true. He said nothing. But he twinkled and looked pleased.

By then my own 'career' in one of the finest rugby-playing provinces of them all had long been terminated. I did play a couple of games for Stroud Nomads. Then again no more postcards came. When I joined the *Stroud News* as a cub reporter the chief printer was Norman Hall, who was captain of Cainscross. They were looking for a scrum-half like me. So were opposing wing-forwards! One game – and I was then in the Cainscross seconds – against Painswick, trampling, hairy, hillside oiks. The referee that day was Bomber Wells, much-respected Gloucestershire cricketer, who loved his rugger in the winters. After half an hour the Bomber blew shrill his whistle and brought the game to a stop. He ordered my battered body to the wing – or else, he said, when I got my breath back, he would send me off. 'Hey, you can't do that!' said my captain. 'I can,' said Bomber. 'It's to save him from further punishment!' I staggered to the touchline as if it were heaven. For the rest of my life I stuck to cricket.

45

The Path of Least Resistance

COL. PHILIP TREVOR

In the days before the First World War, Col. Trevor is taken by surprise
when his daughters and their friends demand to play rugger.
From *Rugby Union Football* (1923).

J UST PRIOR TO the Great War, to be exact in September 1913, I was staying
at a certain seaside place which shall be nameless, when my daughters,
then in various stages of flapperdom, summoned me to a conference. 'Dad,'
they said, 'we must play rugger.' I have been too well trained to offer negative
opposition when woman speaks in unison. Besides, I invariably prefer the path
of least resistance. The thing had obviously got to be done; the only question to
be decided was how best to do it. Fortunately for me, their plans were already
matured. A considerable number of their girl friends who had been playing
hockey with them had also decided that they must play rugger too. There
was a secluded bay round the point, and sand has certain advantages over
turf. The hockey goal-posts could be used, and the marking of the necessary
lines was simple. It was easily explained to me when I came in. I was to get
hold of an oval football. I was also to coach and referee. But my chief duties
were to take all responsibility and to propitiate the infuriated mothers if and
when our secret leaked out. These girls, as they modestly said, hoped to learn
a good deal. Well, I learnt a good deal anyhow. I learnt at any rate that girls
can keep a secret when they want to keep one. Quite early one morning with
hockey sticks in their hands (so easily does flapperdom take to subterfuge) the
conspirators wandered in twos and threes to the bay. The whistle was in my
pocket, and I took the ball down wrapped in a brown paper parcel. We had full
sides (we could have got more than thirty players if we had wanted to), and we
really had a very good first trial. As I said before, I did the learning; and what
a lot I learnt! I do not know quite what the exact definition of a flapper is, but
about a third of the players had their 'hair up'. At our second game most of the
players had their hair up, for bathing-caps were found useful to prevent your
being tackled by your flowing locks. I admit that I found it necessary after
this first game to amend the rules. There was no mistake about the brains,
and certainly there was no mistake about the pluck. I got frightened, and had

to stop the tackling as well as the falling on the ball. Once I had to stop the language. And equally, of course, I got 'back chat' from the young woman I reproved. 'I thought, Major Trevor,' she said to me sarcastically, 'we were to have real rugger. I go to Blackheath every Saturday in winter, and I know what the players say.' The pace at which the game went did not surprise me, for I had played hockey with these young women. But what did surprise and delight me was their pass-giving and the pass-taking. The majority of them seemed to jump to the thing at once, and even in our first game the ball sometimes changed hands accurately without a throw forward three or four times. It was in the matter of the tight scrimmage that the trouble came in. I did not at first penalise for 'foot up in the scrum,' and I am afraid a good many pairs of ankles testified that their owners had played forward that day. We played, in all, three games, and nearly a week passed before a mother got to know what was happening. Then my chief duty came in, but that part of the story is irrelevant. I have not yet discovered how to modify scrimmaging so as to make it suitable or even just possible for girls, though doubtless a more ingenious person than myself will manage to do that. But we hit upon a method of avoiding dangerous tackling. A player was adjudged to be tackled when, while she was in possession of the ball, an opponent placed both hands on her. Some really admirable passing was the result of this rule. The player in possession went full tilt at an opponent, and then at the very last moment tossed the ball to a comrade. You will easily understand that we got some very straight running in consequence. There is no doubt that the average girl who is fond of athletics has the necessary brains for ball games. If my pupils had been, say, boys of twelve or thirteen years of age who had never played rugger before, I feel sure they would not have been so adaptable. Most certainly they would not have been so daring, and I do not think there could have been more pluck. I am delighted to relate that we had no casualties. Nor have I any reason to believe that any of those young women were then, or have been since, any the worse for their three games of rugby football on that stretch of sand.

Several of those young women have since married men who play rugby football, and one of them recently asked me to take her little boy to a rugger match. The father was present at the time. 'He often comes to see me play,' he said. And then he asked me if I believed that a capacity to play rugger could be inherited. I told him that I did, but I think he misunderstood the import of my reply. If when that kid even gets to be appreciably as good a player as his mother he ought to do pretty well. Surely these young women were not just freaks. If in one little village you could find more than thirty girls keen on playing rugby football, how many such could you find in Great Britain? It is not difficult then to account for the ever-increasing popularity of rugby football.

❧

Making His Way

MICHAEL LATHAM

Buff Berry and The Mighty Bongers (1995) tells the story of fly-half John Buff Berry who played for the Lancashire team Tyldesley ('The Mighty Bongers') in the 1890s. He rose from a desperately impoverished childhood to play three times for England.

❧

JOHN BERRY'S LIFE began in humble surroundings in Fellside, a little hamlet just outside Kendal, where he was born on 25 September 1866. After leaving school at the age of eight, by which time he had already acquired the nickname of Buff, he was employed in a tobacco shop. He later worked in a woollen mill as a labourer. With fellow work-mates, young Berry made the most of his rare time off by playing rugby, though not in any organised fashion.

'One winter a lot of us were playing,' he recalled, 'and one of the number who had a bit of money said he would buy a ball if we would pay him back at so much a week. We formed a club called Monument Rovers and eventually we got to playing matches against second teams.'

The Kendal Hornets club was already establishing a solid reputation in rugby circles. 'The Hornets club sprang from a factory team,' Berry explained. 'The factory was known as Castle Mills.' The owner, Mr Frank Wilson, was a sporting enthusiast who encouraged his employees to engage in games, particularly rugby. He placed a field, known as Soldier Field, at their disposal. Later, the club became established at a ground which became known at Mints Feet.

'After Hornets had been going for some time, another team was formed,' Berry continued. 'That team was known by the original name of Castle Mills. One day a benefit match was arranged between the Hornets and Castle Mills and, as half the Hornets team worked at Castle Mills and were going to play with that team, I was asked to fill a vacancy in the Hornets team. I suited them with my play and they kept me on for good afterwards.'

Berry initially appeared in the forwards, but soon made one of the half-back positions his own, forming a celebrated partnership with Billy Cross. By the 1883–4 season, Berry was a regular in the 'Insects' side. It was a good time to be making his way in the game, for Hornets' fixture list was steadily growing in size and prestige, and interest in the game from the townsfolk was mounting with each season.

In an interview for the *St Helens Lantern*, many years later, Cross outlined how popular the rugby game was in Kendal during that era. 'Kendal's only a large village so to say,' he said, 'with a population of about 16,000 and there are plenty fields about to practise on. That makes a great difference as when you have to walk a mile or two to play it knocks the fun out of it. Besides, I couldn't give you an idea of the enthusiasm for football in Kendal. You see there were no other means of amusement there when I was a lad, so we went in heart and soul for football.

'You may think how much we liked it when we lads saved up our pennies for the needful subscriptions. We paid one shilling and sixpence a week each towards the expenses for away matches and one shilling each for home matches. The place being small there were few or no spectators; in fact, if ever we got a £5 gate we nearly jumped out of our jerseys with delight.

'We played for pure love of the game. In those days we had no smart rig-outs – no spiked shoes – no wagonettes – no cabs. We paid our own railway fares and many a time, when we went to play neighbouring villages, we tramped it there and back to save the railway fare of a few coppers.

'Our football shoes were only the ordinary shoes worn every day, with slips of leather temporarily tacked on to the sole. I remember the trouble I had once, at Barrow, to rip them off in order to attend a dance after a game. We couldn't sport bags either but, with our jerseys in a newspaper and a penny bun in our pockets, we travelled along like so many potters. And now can you wonder that lads willing to go through all that should be good players? That's what you may call enthusiasm.'

The Priest with a Passion

ALEX POTTER AND GEORGES DUTHEN

There are a number of extraordinary characters in *The Rise of French Rugby*
(1961), of whom the Abbé Henri Pistre is perhaps the most remarkable; he
even invented a Madame Pistre.

~&~

Igh on the list of France's rugby characters – if not at the top – is
big, jovial Abbé Henri Pistre, parish priest of the village of Noailhac
(population 600), near Castres, southern France, who loved the game to
passion point, yet renounced it. As great match-winning or match-saving feats
have places in the game's history, so should the story of this renunciation, and
of how the abbé did not quite lose his beloved.

In 1921, Henri Pistre, then twenty, was a seminarist in the old cathedral
city of Albi. Soon his army period would begin and, his superior hearing that
young men who won a *brevet militaire* (pre-service fitness test) would not be
displaced for training, encouraged his charges to prepare for it.

Doing this, Henri Pistre, whose sports opportunities had so far been thin,
found that he had been an athlete without knowing it. With no preparation,
and *wearing a soutane*, he jumped five feet five inches. In running kit, he soon
covered the hundred metres in a fifth of a second outside evens.

On sports fields he spent energy as spendthrifts spend money. And he was
built like a rugby forward. So it is hardly surprising (writes Maurice Colinon
in *Pionniers en Soutane*) that in a week or two his army captain, being an old
player, said: 'Pistre, on Thursday you play rugby.'

Pistre played; in the pack; and as though possessed by a demon. Moreover,
this novice performed as though the game was not new to him. So well, in fact,
that next day the captain convoked him. 'Pistre, I speak to you now not as your
captain, but as an official of Albi Rugby Club. I *ask* if you will join us.'

The seminarist-now-soldier was soon playing in Albi's first XV, one of the
best in France. He blossomed into a great player, and was heading for a cap,
when he was demobilised, and returned to the seminary. Several clubs tried to
capture him. 'Leave your studies, play for us, and we will get you a good job.
And you'll be an international. Sign here . . .' Pistre, however, continued his
studies, and played when he wanted to play. And the passion grew.

Then the blow came. He learnt that while a seminarist might play rugby, a priest should not. So with superb stoicism ('the stoicism of the pure rugby player,' said a French writer) he gave it up. He was ordained in Albi Cathedral. Many of his playing friends were there, but only the young men who were ordained with him saw, at the disrobing afterwards, the colours – yellow and black – of Albi Rugby Club. He was wearing a club jersey for the last time. He had worn it this day as a gesture in the renunciation of a love.

That was in 1923, and friends of the Abbé say that, ever since, the Church and rugby have struggled for possession of him, with the Church always winning, though often with little to spare.

The Abbé, however, is allowed to write on the game, and his articles have leading places in the quaintest of sports journals, the weekly *Courrier Sportif du Tarn* (Tarn is his county). Sometimes he writes with a vigour you cannot help associating with old suppressed longings to spend his strength in a pack. It is nearly thirty years since he began writing for the *Courrier Sportif du Tarn*. The paper, born in 1877, was then in very poor health, with a temperature as high as its circulation – just over a hundred. With the Abbé's contributions on his lost love, it rose handsomely, and is now about fifteen hundred.

We sports writers could get a free copy, but we are happy to pay for ours, for it is a reminder of serener days (its make-up hasn't changed since it was born), and the rugby writing is rich and pure. 'You can talk of rugby in many ways,' wrote journalist Yvan Audouard in *Paris-Presse*. 'You can be enthusiastic, even lyrical, with praises, audacious with epithets, violent with denigrations, technical with analyses ... The Abbé Henri Pistre is all these ...'

All these, and more. He called the drab draw (3–3) between France and England in Paris in 1960 a game of smother-ball. 'We don't go to stadiums to see the ball systematically buried. What are undertakers for?' When France beat Ireland in Paris (23–6) two months later and connoisseurs complained that play was too adventurous, he wrote: 'It was gay. A fig for those who called it mad. When our rugby, rid of its old inferiority complex, spreads its wings in the spring sunshine, may we not call it joyful? Why give its young and smiling face a monocle?'

After an extra dull game: 'Is this dingy labour all that we can offer the Youth of France?' And this: 'What we need in our rugby is a freshness, a brightness, and a grace. I hear that Moncla [France's captain] shouted to his braves: "Look out – we're playing in the old style!" Bravo, Moncla! That alone shows you have the makings of a great captain.'

The Abbé suspected certain super-critics of having 'a refrigerator where their bladder ought to be'. He liberally uses phrases such as: 'He clung to the ball as though it was a glass of absinthe or a piece of lobster.' And: 'How could he shine as a forward? It was like expecting a duck to do a trapeze act, or a piece of double-entry book-keeping.'

To hide his identity when he began to write, the Abbé took the extraordinary step, for a Roman Catholic priest, of inventing a wife for himself. Thus, in one of his reports: 'Splendid weather, a good crowd, an excellent cigar, and my wife in a very agreeable mood.' In another article he referred to the imaginary wife as 'Virginie, my gentle dove'. But his style of writing – its imagery and virility – soon led to identification. No one in France writes on the game quite like the Abbé Pistre.

When the French national XVs were getting poor results a few years ago, he wrote: 'Our players eat too much. What can men with paunches do against the bread-boards they send us from Britain?'

But his pen got him into trouble, even in France where, some Europeans say, the libel laws are made of velvet. In a report of a match in 1952 between Castres (the regional team he firmly supports) and Narbonne, he let fly with ink at a referee, saying (among other things):

> His perfumed luggage included a tiny hunting-horn [presumably in place of a whistle] but not the lorgnette indispensable to one so short-sighted. At a welcoming hostelry he refreshed himself after his long journey and, bright-eyed and rosy-cheeked, stepped confidently on to the field, to be greeted with cries of: 'Scoundrel! Knave! Hooligan! Bandit! Give us victory, or tonight we'll hang you on a lamp-post!'
>
> Terrified, the sounder of the hunting-horn lost control. His lofty brow sank almost to the ground, as though he were looking for daisies or buttercups in the December slush ...
>
> ... His brain-box was as empty as the purse of a mendicant friar.

And the Abbé added a postscript:

> I have till now stubbornly defended referees. I have stood by the short-sighted, the short of breath, the clumsy, the unlucky, and the partial ... I cannot support the stupid.

The referee sued for libel, and lost. He appealed, and it looked as though the Abbé had lost. For technical reasons, three further appeals were heard at long intervals, and the result hung fire for six years.

Said the Abbé: 'If I lose, I'll be logical to the end. It's my body they'll have. To prison I'll go. I have no money for damages.'

Said his friends: 'If you go to prison, we'll bring you tasty foods and venerable wines.'

Till 1960 we were never clear how the affair ended; so we wrote to the Abbé, who characteristically replied: 'So you followed what was called the judicial marathon. For six years that referee held with all his teeth to my old soutane. There were not, in this affair, grounds for punishing a cat, let alone for fleecing a priest. I had to pay 20,000 francs [old francs, thus equivalent to about fourteen guineas] and more. Friends helped me . . . You see that the blow has not broken my pen.'

The concluding words refer to the lively way the Abbé continues to write on the game.

He has countless rugby friends. When he was established as a priest, some of them gave him a dinner service wrapped in the colours of the Albi Club. The service is proudly used when he entertains rugby friends. He founded a rugby team in the village of Noailhac. It failed to last, but one of the players turned the Abbé's grief to thankfulness by joining the church choir.

When he was a priest at Castres in 1932 and the town XV was faltering, he became its coach. For two seasons, in the evenings by lamplight, he put the local braves through their paces on an old artillery ground.

From church duties on Sundays he often cycled furiously to the Castres stadium to watch the day's match. Greeted with: 'Have you come straight from church, Monsieur l'Abbé?' he might say: 'Yes, *mon ami*; I rarely see you there.' Nowadays he drives to the Castres ground. If there's a traffic block, gendarmes wave him on. He's part of the establishment. He is respected on all the rugby grounds of France. 'My soutane and hat at first aroused curiosity,' he says. 'Then they were tolerated, then liked, with the simple priest who wears them. I have been applauded by miners. Miners applauding a priest! That's something to boast about . . . Providence made me a rugby player, and that permitted me, later, to do good as a priest.'

When Castres received regional rival Mazamet in a needle match and disturbances were feared, the Abbé made a public appeal:

Tomorrow the supporters of Mazamet will be at the Parc Olympique. I ask the public to give fair play. There is nothing ridiculous about being fond of a team, to be overjoyed by its successes and saddened by its defeats. But these demonstrations should have the right proportions. I will personally be very much hurt if anything regrettable happens tomorrow.

Everything passed off perfectly.

The Abbé Pistre sees most things from the rugby angle. When he goes to Paris, sports journalists like to take him to games other than rugby. Of a tennis champion he said: 'That fellow would make an excellent three-quarter.' Of a boxer: 'His right hook reminds me of that of a prop forward with whom I once had an "explanation".'

Of soccer and billiards: 'They satisfy my mind. Only rugby captures my heart.'

4

THE HARD MEN

Some Match. Some Tactic.
Some Experience . . .

WILLIE JOHN McBRIDE AND PETER BILLS

In *Willie John: The Story of My Life* (2004), McBride tells of being unimpressed
by Ireland's preparation prior to his first international against France in 1963.
McBride played sixty-three times for Ireland and captained the British and
Irish Lions on their successful 1974 tour of South Africa.

❧

WHEN I THINK back to those days, I remember my own early experiences.
For my first game against France at Lansdowne Road, Bill Mulcahy
was captain. It was January 1963 and I was winning only my fifth cap. Bill
was a medical student, so he looked after our welfare as well, because no sub-
stitutions were allowed. You just couldn't go off. If you were dead, you stayed
on to help clutter up the field a bit. Furthermore, you only met up twenty-four
hours before the game and Mulcahy arrived to take the team meeting the
evening before. 'Right,' he said, 'tomorrow we're going to play France. How do
you think we should go about it?'

This invited all sorts of stupid suggestions. One of them came from a so-
called senior player who said, 'Lads, I've played against the French a bit and
I think tomorrow, for the first fifteen or twenty minutes, we should go out
there and try and upset as many of them as we can. If they fall out among
themselves, we'll maybe get a penalty or two or perhaps even score a try. That's
the way to beat them.' Mulcahy promptly slapped his thigh and said, 'Jaysus,
we've got it.' Ireland, everyone felt, were always at their most dangerous when
the tactics were simple. Otherwise we got confused.

So the next day, we trooped into the old wooden shack in a corner of
Lansdowne Road where the teams used to change. That hour before kick-off
in an Irish dressing room was unbelievable. There were guys knocking their

heads against the wall, while others were kicking at benches and doors and working themselves up into a right old frenzy. I'd never seen anything like it. Someone else was running around, saying to anyone who'd listen, 'Has anyone got a spare lace?' It was all highly professional, seriously thought-out preparation for the main event.

Those were the days when you provided everything yourself, apart from the jersey that the Irish Rugby Football Union gave you for the game, so there were guys polishing their boots, putting studs in and smearing Vaseline across their faces to try and look as fit as possible. There was a wee little guy called Charlie McCorry and he was a jack of all trades. If you needed a sponge, a wrench to change your studs, a new lace or whatever, he had everything. The referee knocked on our door about ten minutes before kick-off, wanting to look at our studs. However, someone shouted, 'Don't let the bastard in,' so the ref banging on the door added to the racket and, quite honestly, I couldn't wait to get out of that hell hole. I reckoned the French would be a piece of cake after surviving in that lunatic asylum for the past hour. Besides, we had our secret tactical weapon to upset the French and put us on the road to victory.

Eventually, the referee came back and was admitted. Briefly and grudgingly. Now, with the French already out on the field and the crowd roaring and waiting for our arrival, things had really hotted up in the Irish dressing room. There were guys foaming at the mouth, the sweat was lashing off them, and any stranger wandering into the midst of this horror scene would think he'd stumbled through the back door of a madhouse. The boots trampled anything in their path and we ran out to face the fearsome French.

We get out on to the field and someone blows a whistle. It is a signal, no, an invitation, for all hell to be let loose. Mayhem ensues. I can't remember seeing a ball and, besides, it is irrelevant. You just join the nearest mêlée of players, grabbing, wrestling, swearing, punching and buffeting as you go. Then there is a scrimmage and we know we're quite good at that. We've got a good few hard guys and we're looking forward to that first scrum. It's the traditional test of a team's manhood, whether their forwards can take on and eventually subdue the opposition pack. We stand back, yards apart as you did at that time, and simply charge at the French pack, like rutting stags. No holds barred, not a thought for personal survival or potential injury. This is our first real eyeball-to-eyeball confrontation with the horrible, garlic-smelling, unshaven French forwards and one thing is for sure – we're not going backwards, not by a single inch. There is nothing more humiliating for a forward than to go backwards in a scrum.

Anyway, we crash into each other, French arms grappling with Irish shoulders and vice versa. And then there's the explosion, as if someone has tossed a can of petrol into the midst of this sweating collection of humanity and thrown a match in after it. The whole thing goes up. Irish fists crash into French chins; sometimes Irish fists crash mistakenly into Irish chins. French fingers search out Irish eyes to gouge, a trick to which some French rugby men are as partial as to frogs' legs for dinner. There is widespread shoving, punches whistle past heads that have ducked out of the way and boots connect with shins. Then there's the verbal abuse. 'Ah yer feckin' French pig,' can just about be heard above a stream of Gallic invective, which I don't think is enquiring as to the health of our dear mothers back home. And the referee watches this passable imitation of life and times on the Parisian streets during the French Revolution and does . . . nothing. He never interferes. It's obvious his policy is to enjoy the show and let them sort it out. They'll come to their senses in a moment. Which is a dangerous assumption to make when Ireland plays a game of rugby football.

But in time we do come to our senses, mainly because we're so tired. Hurling punches at people, trying to kick lumps out of them, attempting to wrestle them into submission on the ground is pretty exhausting stuff. In the end, it all comes down to a lot of noise and threats more than anything specific. No one is trying to put back on his missing leg, but there is still one scene of chaos. An Irish forward is lying on the ground, pinned down by a couple of Frenchmen. Eventually, Bill Mulcahy, our brave leader, strides across to him and asks him what's wrong. They manage to drag the two Frenchmen off him, who seem like a couple of hound dogs who've scented the fox and don't intend to quit, and Mulcahy leans over the body of this prostrate Irish colleague. It is Syd Millar, our tight-head prop forward.

'What the matter, Syd?' asks Mulcahy. 'That bastard's bitten me on the arm,' is the response. And sure enough, Mulcahy rolls up Millar's sleeve and there they are – a couple of fang marks, as though Dracula has been visiting the night before. We're all standing around, shocked, appalled. Mulcahy gives him some medical attention. After all, he's a medical student and should know what he's doing. It involves spitting on his own hand and then wiping it across the bitten part of Millar's arm. But his advice is the key point. 'Now Syd, when we go into the next scrum, get hold of yer man's ear and give it a bite.' Millar looks shattered by this pearl of wisdom. Here he is, a proud rugby man of Ireland, and he's been humiliated by this Frenchman, biting his arm and pinning him on the ground at Lansdowne Road in front of 50,000 of his fellow countrymen. Millar looks at his captain with an anguished expression, and says, 'Sure I can't. Me feckin' teeth are in the dressing room.'

Oh, and the master plan that day? Sure, we worked the French up all right. So much so, they won 24–5, by four tries to one. It was their highest score and biggest ever winning points margin in matches against Ireland in Ireland, up to that time. Some match. Some tactic. Some experience.

❧

'Send the b****** off, Ref!': J. D. Clinch

J. B. G. THOMAS

J. D. (Jammy) Clinch, an Irish forward of the 1920s, played 'rough' rugby with a smile, according to this character sketch by the rugby historian J. B. G. Thomas in *Great Rugger Players 1900–1954* (1955).

❧

J. D. CLINCH was immensely strong and enjoyed, more than any other player I know, giving and taking hard knocks in the rough and tumble of forward play. He was a great 'mixer' and like his noted English rival, Tommy Voyce of Gloucester, never complained. In Clinch's opinion it was unfair to give and not receive, and to take on less than two opponents at a time! 'Crash, bang, bang, here comes that broth of a bhoy, Jammy Clinch – if you've got the ball he'll get you!'

Clinch decided that he would become an all-out defender, and pop up in defence wherever he was required. In other words, he was a 'save the situation' man, for he could tackle, handle and kick like the best of full-backs and he was tireless. No forward ever possessed greater courage than Clinch, and opponents respected him, while Welshmen held him in particular esteem. They loved him because he never complained, however hard the struggle was going against him, and because he enjoyed a personal 'feud' with the robust Welsh blind-side wing-forward, Arthur Lemon of Neath. Their duels were the highlights of the Irish–Welsh matches. Clinch must have liked Welshmen, for after the war he settled down in a Monmouthshire Valley and gained a warm place in the hearts of his patients as a cheerful, friendly family doctor.

His broad frame and white elastic headband were the dominating features of Irish forward play for nine seasons. During that time he gained thirty caps and missed only five matches. Invariably he was the toast of Ireland; yet he was not particularly fast and did not move rapidly into attack in the open, but he could bulldoze his way from ten yards out and generally did this with great effect from a heaving maul. Unlike the moderns, Clinch was not a skirmisher; he never stood on the outside of any maul, and the title 'seagull' was never applied to him!

In his excellent book, *Rugger*, Wakefield admits to 'cannibalism' as a result of interference by Clinch. Playing against Ireland, two Irishmen tackled 'Wakers' in a line-out. Clinch joined in to put a 'half-nelson' on the England forward, who could not let the ball go. As he found himself being slowly choked, he had no alternative but to bite Clinch's forearm until he released his vice-like grip. Instead of complaining, Clinch merely grinned and got on with the game! Another story relates how Clinch, playing in the first International match against Wales in 1923, was told by his Welsh opposite number in a line-out, 'Look at your bootlace!' Being, as he says, very innocent, Clinch did so only to receive an uppercut that would have rocked Marciano. However, Clinch goes on to relate that the exponent of the blow was a nice chap really, and they had a very pleasant afternoon beating each other's brains out. The two players have met several times since this occasion, but the Welshman still insists that Jammy was a rough player!

Another story told against the irrepressible Clinch is that when he went for his *viva* in anatomy at Trinity College he was asked to identify a certain bone. 'It's a fibula, sir,' answered Jammy. 'Quite correct. Now is it a right or left fibula?' queried the examiner. Jammy puzzled for some moments, then answered, 'Sir, I would like you to know I am not going for honours!' It is said of Clinch that he was a great hunter and collector of trophies, which he hoarded in his flat in Northumberland Road, Dublin. It is said that in one instance he brought back a young tree from a famous boulevard in Paris for his mother, digging it up one evening under cover of darkness when no one was near.

Welshmen could always recognise him by the elastic band he wore around his head, and Jammy says that he did not like a skull cap, but found that his ears were being torn continually, so he adopted Jock van Druten's idea of wearing an elastic headband, which took the strain and proved cooler than a scrum cap. A few years after his last International match against South Africa in 1931–2, he resumed his medical studies at the Royal College of Surgeons in Dublin, and amidst great delight qualified in 1937 and finally settled into the noble profession.

His proudest moment was when he trotted out with the Irish team to play at Swansea in 1930, to be greeted with a shout from the crowd 'Send the b***** off, Ref!' Jammy thought it was very nice to be remembered after an interval of four years. He lost four jerseys in the 1926 match against Wales at Swansea! There is no doubt that Clinch was one of the most colourful characters in Irish football between the wars. He played in an era which contained many personalities, and he was outstanding among them and his rivals from the other countries.

'Big Arth'

ROGER McGOUGH

Roger McGough is a poet, broadcaster, essayist and children's author.

Big Arth from Penarth
was a forward and a half.
Though built like a peninsula
with muscles like pink slagheaps
and a face like a cheese grater
he was as graceful and fast
as a greased cheetah.

A giraffe in the lineout
a rhino in the pack
he never passed forward
when he should've passed back
and once in possession
slalomed his way
through the opposition.

And delicate?
Once for a lark
at Cardiff Arms Park
Big Arth
converted a soft-boiled egg
from the halfway line.

No doubt about it, he was one of
the best players in the second team.

PoW Place Kicker: 'Okey' Geffin

CHRIS GREYVENSTEIN

Born in 1921 to a Lithuanian Jewish family who emigrated to South Africa,
Geffin, a prop forward and placekicker, fought in the Second World War
but was captured after the Battle of Tobruk in 1941 and imprisoned as
a PoW in Toruń, Poland. From *Springbok Rugby:
An Illustrated History* (1995).

IT WAS ADOLF Hitler's birthday and as a special treat the commandant of the prisoner-of-war camp at Toruń, Poland, granted everybody an extra hour in bed. The Führer's birthday could not have been better timed as far as the South African and New Zealand inmates of the camp were concerned. They needed the extra rest because the first rugby trials were scheduled to be played later in the day. For some time the main topic of conversation had been a proposed 'Test series' between the rugby world's two keenest rivals. Bill Payn, the 1924 Springbok forward, was the main organiser and he and Peter Pienaar, son of the 1921 Springbok captain Theo Pienaar, and Billy Millar Jnr, son of the 1912 South African captain, very quickly discovered that there was more than enough talent among their fellow prisoners.

The senior medical officer in the camp had given permission for the games to be played, but he added a warning that he would soon put a stop to the activities if 'any player walks into hospital with a broken neck'. A field was marked off with yellow clay lines on the vast sandy parade ground and with army boots considered too lethal for the match, the players played with bare feet.

One of the most enthusiastic players among the South Africans was a burly Jewish boy born twenty-two years before, less than a good touch-kick's distance away from the Ellis Park rugby ground, the stadium where he once saw Gerry Brand in action and promptly acquired a healthy dose of hero worship. His fellow prisoners knew him as 'Ox' Geffin and his raw strength and accurate bare-footed kicking made him one of the stars in the many rough-and-ready matches to follow.

Geffin learnt a lot in those matches and it could well be, as has often been written, that he practised his placekicking on the mass grave in which thousands of Nazi-executed Poles were buried, but the truth is that he was already a promising member of Johannesburg Pirates by the time he donned the khaki uniform. It was at the Pirates club that Freddie Turner first spotted his potential and it was Turner who gave him his first practical lesson in the art of placekicking. Geffin was fortunate that he encountered a coach as intelligent as Turner, whose own style was completely different. Turner used to lift the ball very high while Geffin's kicks had a low trajectory. Instead of trying to change the boy's style, Turner merely helped him to make the most of it. As an under-nineteen player Geffin once succeeded with twelve out of thirteen conversions and he was obviously already on his way to bigger things when the war intervened.

When the hostilities finally ceased 'Ox' became known as 'Okey' (nobody really knows how or why) and he was soon a regular frontranker in the powerful Transvaal pack under Jan Lotz in the late 1940s. Throughout his career Geffin never followed the flight of the ball until after his follow-through had brought his boot in line with his vision. He believed that this was the secret of timing and accuracy. Geffin must be the only Springbok never to have an official Christian name. Everybody accepted it to be Aaron but on his birth certificate there was nothing but a blank space until he had it rectified years later. Okey always had his own explanation for this. 'When my father went to register my birth and they asked him for my Christian names he must have said: "He's a Jewish boy! He's got no Christian names!"'

But whether he was 'Ox', 'Okey' or 'Aaron', this bull-necked Transvaler, with Muller and Brewis, filled the leading roles in the first post-war Test series when the Springboks had to defend their rugby crown against the All Blacks.

Identity and Brutality in the South-West: Jean 'Le Sultan' Sébédio

PHILIP DINE

Sébédio played eleven times for France from 1913 to 1922, his international appearances restricted by the First World War. Nicknamed 'Le Sultan' because he had fought in Syria, he was once arrested for singing 'The Marseillaise' in a Dublin pub with Irish independence supporters prior to an international game against Ireland.

A BASQUE FROM THE fishing port of Saint-Jean-de-Luz, Jean 'Le Sultan' Sébédio was an excellent *pelota* player as well as a hugely talented rugby forward. A member of the French national team either side of the Great War – indeed, he was the first working-class player to be selected for *le XV de France* – Sébédio was celebrated as *une force de la nature*, being immensely strong despite his only medium size. Having played for both Tarbes and Biarritz before the war, he was mobilised and fought in the Syrian campaign (where he earned his nickname), before embarking on what was effectively a second playing career with Béziers briefly, and then famously with Carcassonne.

It was as a trainer that Sébédio took the Lézignan side to the 1929 final with Quillan, in spite of a training regime that was unusual to say the least: 'Having already lost a good deal of his vitality as a result of frighteningly excessive drinking, he cultivated his persona by sitting in the middle of the pitch with a long whip and a wide sombrero, making his players run round him like circus horses.' Sébédio's incarnation in his own person of the structural linkage between drink and rugby in the Aude and the rest of the Languedoc is particularly striking, with other centres for both activities established in Narbonne, in Béziers and, indeed, throughout the ancient *provincial narbonensis*, where the Romans had first planted vines. However, it was Sébédio's close association with violence, and particularly his ability to intimidate visiting players and referees, that is, paradoxically, most fondly remembered by French rugby's chroniclers. So, in his colourful collection of portraits of *Seigneurs et forçats du rugby* (Lords and Slaves of Rugby), Henri Garcia tells with relish how visiting supporters descending from trains

at Lézignan under the Sultan's reign were greeted with the cry '*Lézignan!*
Lézignan la Matraque! Tout le monde descend!' ('Lézignan! Lézignan the Cosh!
Everyone out!'). Garcia also enjoys telling how Sébédio kept a human skeleton
hanging in the referee's changing room, with a whistle stuck between its jaws,
and would inform the concerned official casually that it was 'nothing to worry
about, just the last referee to give a penalty against Lézignan'. However, it is
as one of the stars of Garcia's picaresque *Contes du rugby* that 'the Sultan' really
comes into his own. Depicted in his heyday as a player with the Association
Sportive Carcassonnaise, Sébédio is as memorable a figure in the bar-room
as he is on the pitch. Whether engaging in terrifying post-match drinking
competitions with predictably cowed opponents, or refusing to accept the
decisions of intimidated match officials, Sébédio is depicted as a genuinely
fearsome figure, but also, crucially, an admirable and even a lovable one. In
Garcia's words:

> The Sultan feared no man, either on the pitch or at the bar. Jean
> Sébédio was an exceptional being. He could play in virtually every
> position in the team, such was his strength, agility and skill. All those
> who knew him are unanimous in asserting that they have rarely seen
> a player of his calibre.
>   . . . Such a man was worth his weight in gold to a team, but for
> referees, he was a nightmare. In Carcassonne, on the pitch at the
> Pépinière ground, the Sultan was the only master after God and a
> long way ahead of the referee.

The undisputed master in his *fief*, Sébédio epitomises the *méridional* cult of
the strong-man. Moreover, he is very much a patriarch in its original sense,
the head of the clan or tribe, and as such an iconic figure in the culture of the
south-west.

❧

Men, Rough Men and Rugby:
Blair Swannell

HERBERT M. MORAN

Swannell, a forward, played seven times for British Isles teams in 1899
and 1904. After a tour to Australia, he settled in Sydney and played once for
Australia against New Zealand in 1905. Moran, a prop, was captain of the
1908–9 Australian touring team to the British Isles, playing in one Test.
He left the tour before it was completed to resume his medical studies.
From *Viewless Winds* (1939).

❧

BLAIR SWANNELL WAS, for a number of years, a bad influence in Sydney
football, and also incidentally a greatly over-estimated player. His
conception of rugby was one of trained violence. He himself kept in perfect
condition; this alone enabled him to conceal his slowness on the field. He was
an expert, however, in the art of when and how to wheel or screw a scrum; a
manoeuvre in which few Australian forwards have much experience. But he
had no enlightened ideas about sport and used to teach schoolboys all sorts
of tricks and tactics which were highly objectionable. In appearance he was
extremely ugly but, like Wilkes in the eighteenth century, he could talk his
face away in half an hour. He was popular with the fair sex; men, generally,
disliked him.

I played with and against him on a number of occasions. The last time we
were in opposition was on the Sydney Cricket Ground. Although we were
friendly, he persisted in screwing the scrum towards my side. I, as breakaway,
had then to go down on the ball, whereupon he would kick me on any exposed
part of my back. This was his conception of the correct game. Subsequently
when he had taken a ball on the line-out (a rare thing for him, for he was not
proficient in this branch of play) I tackled him very hard and he resented it.
He was off his balance at the time and hit the ground violently. For the rest
of the game after that he continued to screw the scrum to my side even when
it seemed to be the wrong manoeuvre for his own team. My back was black
and blue from his attentions. At the end of the game, as we all walked off the
field, he looked across at me, a much younger player, to see how I had taken

it all. Then he called out: 'Are you satisfied?' 'Perfectly,' I replied. After which he invited me to have a glass of beer with him; a signal honour, for he was not given to treating.

In life, as on the football field, Swannell gave no quarter, and asked for none. We, less mature men, stood somewhat in awe of him. There were quite a number of players in those matches who terrorised us somewhat: they were much older, much harder types. One of them used to wear a terrible fringe of hair low down on his forehead. He had the habit of coming round the scrum when the referee was not looking and of swinging his fists and his feet. The University players detested him: he seemed a sort of ogre. Then for twenty-five years I did not see him until there was a famous reunion of veteran players. By then mildness had descended upon him and at that gathering of veterans he looked so like the little wife-intimidated man who took round the plate at a suburban church I knew. He seemed also to have shrunken. I found myself looking at him with such open-mouthed surprise that he growled: 'Did you think I was dead?' I laughed. He looked so harmless. I couldn't tell him I was wondering if this was the bogey man to whom we attributed all the vices of rough and unsporting play. In a similar way most of us disliked and somewhat feared Swannell. He went in 1905 to New Zealand with an Australian rugby team, and in that land of vigorous football his unpleasing face suffered further casualty from a foeman's boot. He got there what he had often given elsewhere. There was no preciosity in his workmanship. He was a hard, virile, unsympathetic type, but a man.

In the end he wore an Australian uniform as stubbornly as he had worn an Australian jersey. He was early in the field, and found his end storming the goal on that April morning at Gallipoli. I can imagine him rushing forward with a frown on that ugly face with its scar from a New Zealand boot. He is still there holding on. When his death became known to the troops, it was rumoured that his own men had shot him down. They did not like his domineering English manner or the way that, in speaking, he clipped off the end of his words. But the story of his being shot from behind was just somebody's canard.

It was always expected of a Roman emperor that he should die on his feet. Swannell, no doubt, thought a footballer should perish following on. His hard-visaged comrades said he died with the ruling passion strong upon him: still putting in the boot. Be that as it may: through sacrifice he passed to transfiguration. The hard porcelain of his spirit had a richer glaze than we had previously perceived; it was the love of country. For me who knew him well this is his epitaph: He never hung out of a ruck.

᠊᠊᠊᠊᠊᠊᠊᠊᠊᠊᠊᠊᠊᠊᠊᠊᠊

The Gentle Laying-on of Hands

E. B. OSBORN

This extract from an essay *The Game* was contributed by E. B. Osborn, a journalist, author and editor, to *The Game Goes On* (1936) edited by H. B. T. Wakelam.

᠊᠊᠊᠊᠊᠊᠊᠊᠊᠊᠊᠊᠊᠊᠊᠊᠊

THERE ARE TEAM-GAMES, such as hockey and lacrosse, in which there is little or no man-to-man contact, the necessary technique comprising ball-control, passing, and as much pace as possible. Except for robust shoulder-charging, which is only seen today in Varsity and school matches (some referees seem to think professional players are too brittle to endure it), Soccer would come into this category. Then there are the personal sports, boxing and wrestling, in which vigorous man-to-man contact is the technical basis. But rugger combines the attractiveness of either type of game, together with the spice of peril without which no sport is really worthwhile. That is why it must rank as the greatest of all the team-games invented by man.

In its unorganised form it was indeed a perilous pastime. In Tudor days matches were played on seasonal holidays between rival townships, in which a small ball, called the *knappan*, was used that was never intended to be kicked. These were sometimes thousand-a-side affairs, and the ball might be carried towards either goal even by mounted combatants. The player who was tackled in possession and refused to 'deal the *knappan*,' as the phrase ran, could be persuaded to do so by means of fragments of rock or heavy cudgels, which must have been harder than the hardest things in the modern game, i.e. the boots of Scottish international forwards. The loose mauls must sometimes have justified the description of them by Sir Thomas Elyot, a contemporary witness, as 'nothing but beastlike furie and extreme violence, whereof procedeth hurte'. A Welsh friend of ancient lineage (I dare say his long genealogical scroll has the inscription halfway down: 'About this time the Flood occurred') is proud of the fact that this aboriginal form of handball was most popular in Pembrokeshire and other parts of Wales. That is why, he believes, rugger became the Welshman's national winter game. Perhaps it also explains why Welsh forward-play is at times 'just a little zealous,' to use a Blackheathen's entertaining euphemism. The Puritan Stubbes, though he began fairly enough by describing the ball-play he knew as 'a friendlie kind of fight', goes on to accuse the players of employing many a 'bloody and murthering practice', such as tackling an opponent so that he pitches on his nose on hard stones. After Stubbes's condemnation the criticism of Sir William Davenant that football 'is not very conveniently civil' seems mild to the point of absurdity. Carew, who tells us about seventeenth-century football in his native Cornwall, is the only one of those witnesses who sees that such exercise hardens a man and puts courage into his heart 'to meet an enemy in the face'. And he also admits that the injuries received, even if bones be broken, were taken in good part, 'and never attorney or coroner troubled for the matter'. In the twenty-a-side rugger deliberate hacking was permitted, and a relation of mine was a forward in the first England v. Scotland match used to show the marks on his shins of wounds received under the barbarous old rules. Indeed, he was proud of these honourable scars, which he kept to the day of his death in a green old age. Hacking and tripping up a runner were wisely made illegal. But the appeal of the game would be weakened if attempts were made to rule out the robust play which is not likely to injure the man in decent condition. As it is, the code is far too complicated – as perplexing, indeed, as an income-tax form with the cryptic directions for filling it up. When he orders a scrum, there are at least twenty things for the unfortunate referee to think of! How many internationals, who have been playing since they were small boys, could score 50 out of a 100 marks in an examination on the rules?

Fortunately, when in charge of a match played in the right spirit, the referee ignores minor infringements. If he did not, the game would be just one long boresome blast on his whistle! Like the successful public-school master, he must take care not to see too much. I have heard soft-hearted people (almost always non-players) complain that there is too much roughness in the game nowadays, and suggest that legislation to suppress it is urgently required. I hope that nothing of the kind will ever be done. To take one point, of which the non-player is unaware, the only way to stop dirty work, which can seldom be seen by the referee, is to put the fellow guilty of it out of action. Such cases very seldom occur, but every experienced player must be able to recall the effective laying-out of a systematic offender by means that were certainly 'not very conveniently civil', to repeat Davenant's polite phrase.

The 'gentle laying-on of hands' is an indispensable part of the glory of a game which is good to watch, better still to play. Is there any greater delight than a flying tackle such as that which Obolensky, swooping out of the nowhere into the here, brought off on Rawlence in the last Oxford v, Cambridge match? To me, a patriotic Oxonian, it was as memorable as the historic tackling of an unstoppable three-quarter (W. E. Maclagan at full gallop) by the unpassable back (H. B. Tristram) which happened nearly fifty years ago. The hero of that thrilling episode remembers every minute detail of his plan for securing both man and ball. Fifty years hence, I hope, the fleet-footed Russian will as clearly recall just how he saved what seemed a certain try for Cambridge. I can remember scores of 'the walk into my parlour, said the spider to the fly' tackle, of which the famous English full-back, Gamlin, was such a subtle master. Subtle, because the man with the ball felt somehow obliged to fall into the trap.

Hard tackling is such a joyous business for the real worker, who never plays to the gallery, that he remembers with special pleasure some of the matches which were most disappointing to the spectator. I myself was a front-row forward of no particular distinction who has really no right to a place among the many famous contributors to this symposium. But I can say this for myself – nobody ever had a greater affection for the game or got more pleasure from doing his job, without giving or expecting quarter.

. . . Later on, I had exhilarating experiences of rugger as played in Lancashire and Yorkshire before the formation of the Rugby League, which deprived the orthodox game of its richest recruiting-ground for the best type of forward. More than once the English pack included as many as five Yorkshire scrummagers, men of great mass and momentum, and was able to wear down the toughest Scottish combination. Having been at a soccer school (long since converted to the nobler form of football), I could play my part in a close-dribbling rush, which was then a favourite stratagem in the north. There was always a veritable 'Battle of the Roses' when my Lancashire team crossed the Pennines to play in Yorkshire. I remember how one of the best Lancashire forwards, who might have got his cap for England but for getting permanently crocked, used to see us off and give us a parting word of advice. 'When you're tackling them Tykes,' he said, 'don't put 'em down same as I put down my little Jessie. Fair bury 'em, lads!' There would be plenty of scrapping to amuse the crowd. You were always liable to be tackled good and hard when not in possession. One of the mightiest forwards ever capped for England, a genial giant with a face like a ruddy harvest moon, once flattened me out while the ball was soaring away into touch. Having gathered myself up, I told him what I thought of him and Yorkshire, and he replied with a huge grin: 'Eh, la-ad, but tha' was leukin' at t'ball.' A little later we had a scrap in a line-out, and, having learnt how to punch, I got my own back. How strange it is that I can recall those ruthless rough-and-tumbles more vividly than the cricket matches in which I enjoyed a long spell of hard hitting or took a number of wickets.

As Hard as a Miner's Toecap

NICK BISHOP AND ALUN CARTER

John 'The Perk' Perkins was a second row forward who played for Pontypool from 1974/75 to 1986/87 and was capped eighteen times for Wales. From *The Good, The Bad and The Ugly: The Rise and Fall of Pontypool RFC* (2013).

A s GRAHAM PRICE remembers: 'The Pontypool forwards, especially in the '70s, were as hard as a miner's toecap. We were never big, but we had heart. John Perkins, "the Perk", was a perfect example. Only six foot one and fifteen stone, but the dominant lock of his era in Wales. All the so-called hard men were not hard men, in my opinion. They were either bullies or hit-and-run merchants who would check the ref wasn't looking, take their shot and bugger off out of there. Perk was the opposite: if he was going to take a shot, he was also going to stand up and take anything that was coming back at him. 'Never back down' could have been Perk's motto and it applied to other genuinely hard men like Gloucester's Mickey Burton.

'I remember once Robert Paparemborde telling me how – on some invitational tour – Perky had literally thrown himself in the way of a blind-sider intended for the French prop and taken it himself. While Perk was rolling around dazed on the ground, "Papa" was thanking him and smiling. The Basques play with a huge sense of family and he knew the value of what Perky had done, even if the Perk was probably regretting it!

'The Perk would put his body on the line for the whole eighty minutes for the team; he never shirked a job that had to be done – while the hit-and-run merchants would be out of the game on the fringes, awaiting retribution for their felonies! They knew they'd marked their own card and you'd be looking for them, so they kept out of the way for the rest of the match.

'Perky would give as good as he got – "I've got two stitches in me for every one I've put in someone else," he'd say – and it was true. I can remember taking him up to the hospital in Nevill Hall, Abergavenny, after he'd been kneed in the kidneys from the opening kick-off in one game. To me, he was real Pontypool. He was red, white and black to the core.'

Terry Cobner takes up the story: 'Perk didn't really care about anything except rugby. He must have had six or seven jobs while he played for Pontypool. He was a miner at the Big Pit, he was a chippie, he was a travelling sales rep and he was a teacher. The minute any of them interfered with his rugby, or even threatened to do so, he'd let it go.

'When he was a rep, he had a call from his manager: "Perk, there's a bloke down in Llanelli who's eager to do a deal. Get down there and close it." So Perk put his blazer on and his Pontypool tie and jumped in his car. When he arrived, they started talking about rugby and it went on for hours. Finally, Perk said, "So what do you want to order?" The bloke was taken aback and replied, "Oh, I don't really want to order anything now, I just wanted to talk to you about rugby. Come back in the spring." Perky was fuming: "What do you mean, come back in the spring? I'm not a f***ing cuckoo!"'

The Perk was not the tallest second row by any means, but he was the person to whom we threw when in trouble. He was an agile jumper at the front and he was as tough as they come, with a left jab that he used as a clubbing tool to test the will to fight of all-comers throughout the eighty minutes. But he'd prefer to call that lob to the front of the line-out early in the game, whack his opponent in the bollocks as he soared to make the catch and *then* get on with the job of winning the ball in peace and quiet for the rest of the match. That was the protocol.

The Old Master: Boy Louw

CHRIS GREYVENSTEIN

Boy Louw won eighteen caps for South Africa from 1928–38,
usually playing as a prop forward.
From *Springbok Rugby: An Illustrated History* (1995).

❧

Matthys Michael (Boy) Louw, in particular, became a legend in his own lifetime. A man of enormous physical strength, Louw also had an instinctive flair for the game and he understood the fundamentals down to the most minute details. Near the end of his career as a player, Louw became known as 'The Old Master' and there can be no more apt nickname for this phenomenal player. Boy Louw was a hard, relentless competitor who stood no nonsense from anyone, but it was his brain and not his brawn that earned him such a special place in our rugby history. Born on 2 February 1906 on a farm in the district of Wellington in the heart of the Boland, Boy was the fifth of ten brothers and four sisters. One of his brothers died while still very young, but the other nine all played senior rugby. Boy and Fanie became Springboks and four of the other brothers progressed to interprovincial level.

Boy Louw took his rugby seriously and not even Bennie Osler ever tried to overrule him in a match. Danie Craven tells the story of how Osler once called for the ball from a scrum during the wet and windswept test against Scotland in 1932.

'Hold, and play with the forwards!' Louw countermanded his captain's order from the front row. But Osler again commanded Craven to pass. This time Louw whipped his head from the forming scrum and snorted:

'Nonsense with you, Bennie! We're keeping it up front!' In fact he used a word much stronger than 'nonsense' and Osler saw no point in further argument.

On another occasion he told a captain: 'You make the speeches, I'll lead the pack!' and that is the way it was.

Louw has often fought a losing battle with tongue-twisters and his malapropisms have kept several generations of players amused. Some of the stories told about him are no doubt apocryphal, but it is a fact that he did sometimes produce a somewhat mixed-up version of what he really intended to say.

One of the most delightful anecdotes is the one Craven told of the time Boy and his pack were battling mightily in a match when Springbok centre Johnny Bester not only dropped hard-earned possession, but stood rooted on the spot and did not fall back to recover the situation. As Boy ran past Bester, he slapped him on the rump and reprimanded:

'Hey, do you think you have bought this ground of plot?'

Craven also vouches for the fact that it was indeed Boy who once looked at a sloppy line-out and said:

'Why you stand so crooked? Can't you stand in a straight stripe?'

Throughout his long international career, which included eighteen Tests, Louw was invariably the man the half-backs and three-quarters turned to whenever they were the victims of dirty tactics from the opposing forwards. Boy's retribution was always swift and merciless. To quote Danie Craven: 'In one of the matches in New Zealand in 1937 there was a forward wearing a number-12 jersey who kept on climbing in on the wrong side of the loose scrums. I dealt with him twice, but he persisted and each time Mauritz van den Berg would ask me who it was and I would answer that it was number 12 again. Finally it was all too much for Boy. "What's wrong with you fellows today?" he asked and at the next opportunity the offending number 12 came flying out of the loose scrum to land at my feet, one eye already coming up like a balloon. Then I heard Boy's voice: "Mr Ref, you can blow your whistle now, number 12 is off!"'

5

THE WHISTLE BLOWERS

The Young Man's Game

ALEC WAUGH

An extract from one of a collection of essays,
On Doing What One Likes (1926).

❧

EVERY RUGGER MAN in the United Kingdom knows that the game is only worth the playing as long as he can trust his opponents to keep within the spirit of the law.

That they should keep within the letter of the law would be a vain and unprofitable expectation, vain because only one player in ten has ever read the rules; unprofitable because it is unlikely that the referee will be conducting the game in accordance with the latest rulings of the Rugby Union. The laws are altering every season, and the average rugger player simply cannot be bothered to keep in touch with them. If in cold blood, in an examination room, he were asked what a forward should do when he is collared with the ball, he would answer probably correctly. But in hot blood when he is himself that outraged forward, he cannot pause to think whether the Rugby Union has ceased to allow him to do now, a thing it allowed him to do last season. He just does what he always has done. And if a free kick is given against him, he bears no malice. He shakes his head. 'Ah! well,' he says, 'so they are playing by those rules today, are they? I must try not to do that again.' The rugger man is aware that there are certain broad principles. He knows, for instance, that you may not stand offside and wait for your friends to bring the ball along to you. He expects when he does that to be penalised. But he does not pretend to know the subdivisions of the rules, nor usually does the referee.

. . . After a couple of months of club football, one comes to regard the rules as something relative to the temperament and training of the particular referee; one sets out at once, preferably in midfield, to discover by what edition of the rules the game is to be played, and then 'one acts accordin''; one gets some bad shocks sometimes in the first five minutes, but soon one is in one's stride.

And indeed the rules themselves are a somewhat haphazard business. Were they not they would hardly be changed so frequently. In no other game is so much freedom given to the referee. He does not exact the law, he interprets it. The word 'intentional' occurs in the rules a good many times, and on the referee's interpretation of what is and what is not intentional depends the awarding of a scrum or a free kick. In no other game, I believe, is this distinction made. In soccer, if a man is in front of the ball when it is kicked and there are not two defenders between him and the goal, he is offside and there is a free kick, and there is no more to it. In rugger a man may be offside inadvertently because the scrum has wheeled, or he may be lazy, and having overrun the ball been content to wait for the other forwards to bring it up to him, or again he may be deliberately attempting to take an unfair advantage of his opponents; the fact that he is offside is of less importance than the manner in which he has come to be offside. It is for the referee to decide under which category the player's offence falls.

That word 'intentional' is the most important of the three or four odd thousand words that go to the construction of the rules. It is a key to the spirit of the game; it shows why the game can be played only by those who are playing it for its own sake simply; shows why there can be no professionals; shows also perhaps why it is that eighty per cent of the men at an International are present or past public schoolboys; why the rugger world has come to be a kind of a family party.

Hacked Off at the Head

HUW RICHARDS

The result of the first ever international (Scotland v. England, 1871)
swung on a disputed try awarded by Dr Almond, one of the umpires,
as referees were then called. He later gave a revealing insight into his
decision-making process, possibly still valid for today's referees.
From *A Game for Hooligans: The History of Rugby Union* (2006).
Huw Richards is a journalist, historian and author of
many books and articles on rugby.

❧

ENGLAND TRAVELLED OVERNIGHT by train to play two halves of fifty
minutes at Raeburn Place, Edinburgh Academicals' ground, in front of a
crowd variously estimated at between two and four thousand, whose shillings
were collected by John MacDonald, enthusiasm undimmed by memories
of interminable schoolboy scrummaging. Wearing all white with a red rose
on their shirts, England confronted a Scottish team clad in blue jerseys and
cricket flannels. It proved a spirited contest. Scottish forward Robert Irvine
recalled, 'There were a good many hacks-over going on and as blood got up it
began to be muttered, "Hang it, why not have hacking allowed? It cannot be
prevented; far better have it."' (The England captain) Stokes and his Scottish
counterpart Francis Moncrieff were unable to decide, but umpire Hely
Hutchinson Almond, headmaster of Loretto College, warned he would not
continue if hacking were allowed. It was not his last significant decision.

Guillemard, full-back for England and doubtless participating enthusiastically in that early outbreak of hacking, recalled, 'The match was very evenly contested until half-time, after which the combination of the Scotsmen, who knew
each other's play thoroughly, and their superior training began to tell a tale.'

From a scrum five yards out, the Scots drove forward and grounded the
ball. Amid vociferous English protests, Almond gave the try, and Malcolm
Cross kicked the decisive goal. Scotland were to claim a further try, while
Reginald Birkett of Clapham Rovers, who later took his club's hybridity to the
logical conclusion of also playing soccer for England, crossed for the visitors.
Neither, though, scored any points, as both conversions were missed – under
the rules of the time, unconverted tries were worth nothing.

England's anger at a score which would not have been allowed under their rules contributed to their downfall. Scottish practice was that only the captain was allowed to appeal to the umpire. Almond would write many years later that, had England followed this practice, 'I should have understood that the point raised was that the ball had never been fairly grounded in the scrummage but had got mixed up among Scottish feet or legs.' It was, he conceded, impossible to know where a ball was amid the scrums of the twenty-a-side era. But amid multiple vociferations, he could not find out exactly what the problem was. In any case, he concluded magnificently, 'When an umpire is in doubt, I think he is justified in deciding against the side which makes most noise. They are probably in the wrong.'

The Boy Referee

DEREK BEVAN WITH OWEN JENKINS

Before he turned to refereeing, going on to control the 1991 World Cup final,
Derek Bevan played as a flanker. Here he recalls an incident when he himself
fell foul of the referee, before telling what happened when he was in charge of a
match involving one of his heroes. From *The Man in the Middle* (2001).

ON ONE OCCASION the Vardre were playing against Llandybie in a Cup game. They had a very talented outside half called Gwyn Ashby who had run rings around us earlier in the season. So the order went out for me to put one in early on. Irrespective of what he would do, he was going to have one! So I did exactly that and it was going to be late and painful. It's an awful thing to say but it was our way of counteracting skill! He kicked ahead and I got him. It was a tremendous midriff challenge and I heard the wind surging out from him. He'd been hurt. The referee was the late Denzil Lloyd from Nantyffyllon who was on the international panel. Like all experienced referees he didn't follow the kick but glanced behind him and caught me in the act. He made sure that Ashby was okay and came for me. He told me that he knew exactly what I was doing and gave me a final warning. This meant that I had to tread very carefully for the remaining seventy-five minutes. Ashby could either be lacking in bravery and keep one eye out for me, which meant I would have won our little game within a game. But he did the exact opposite and made a complete fool of me for the rest of the game. He dummied me, went around me when he pleased with his superior pace. Once he held out the ball and taunted me. Like an idiot I went for it but he then danced around me and I could hear the laughter from the Llandybie supporters. The truth is that the first time I touched him was when I'd hit him late and the second time that I'd touched him was to shake his hand after the game. I'd brought it on myself.

My hero was Terry Cobner. He was leading the Pontypool pack, for which I had a tremendous respect. Early in my career in the top flight, when I was given a fixture between Pontypool and Bristol on a Tuesday night I really hoped that Cobner would be playing. I had never refereed at Pontypool Park before. Mike Rafter, the England flanker, was the Bristol captain. I called the two skippers out before the game and shook their hands. 'Cob' wished me all the best and welcomed me to Pontypool. He was calling me 'Sir' during the game. If I had to sort one of his players out he told me 'Leave it to me Sir'. I thought that this was great. He was doing my work for me. At the end of the match which Pontypool won, 'Cob' shook my hand and thanked me. He told me there'd always be a welcome in Pontypool for people like me. I thought that this was a great day and that I had obviously performed well. Rafter then came on to me. He also thanked me and said 'I'm going to thank the other referee now – Terry Cobner.' In the clubhouse afterwards Rafter came up to me once again and said 'I hope you didn't mind me saying that at the end of the game?' 'Not at all,' I replied, 'I can take a joke.' 'But I wasn't joking,' he said. 'I was very serious. Almost every fifty-fifty situation you gave it to them.' Cobner had been so clever, he'd worked me a treat. The next time I went to Pontypool, Cobner started the same thing again. But this time I turned to him and said 'When I want your help skipper, I'll ask for it.' Cobner grinned. He'd been tumbled, the boy referee had grown up.

❧

A Wild Swing

NICK BISHOP AND ALUN CARTER

In this extract, Graham Price, the Pontypool prop and one of the most celebrated forwards of his era, tells of the change in refereeing attitudes in the 1970s. From *The Good, The Bad and The Ugly: The Rise and Fall of Pontypool RFC* (2013).

❧

IT WAS A brutal game in the '70s. If the referee didn't see something, then it didn't happen. Because they were all on the circuit, the refs knew the guys who were looking for trouble and they knew the ones who weren't interested in it. They would monitor the reactions of those groups during the game and tailor their refereeing to it.

Whereas nowadays refs will yellow- or even red-card anyone they see committing foul play, back then the refs would see retaliation for what it was. If a player who was known to belong to the non-violent faction got enraged and threw a punch or a kick, the ref would usually ignore it and look for the root cause. The most violent or psychotic blokes also tended to be those endowed with the most sheer animal cunning, so they knew the situations in which they were unlikely to get caught!

Mickey Burton told me a story once about how he got belted in a game against Pontypool and took a wild swing at the man he thought was the culprit. There was a prompt response on the whistle from Ken Rowlands, who called Burton across in his most severe school-teacher manner.

He stood there for about two minutes, wagging his forefinger in Mickey's face in front of the bank. I thought he was going to poke his eye out. Mickey told me afterwards that Ken had said, 'Well, I know there must have been a reason why you took a swing, Mike, and I have a fair idea who did it, but I have to make an example of you in front of these b*****ds.' The finger wagged even harder. '. . . So I'm going to stand here giving you a telling-off and give them a penalty.' As Rowlands sent Burton away like a naughty schoolboy into the corner, he muttered under his breath, 'You've earned yourself one punch in retaliation. Make it count!'

A Necessary Evil

RON MITCHELL

If players sometimes feel less than positive towards referees, referees can feel the same about their assessors. From *So Why Did You Become a Referee?* (2004).

❧

ASSESSORS ARE A necessary evil. Discuss. Rather like an A-level question. The following chapter is not meant to be an A-level answer.

An assessor is a dedicated referee who, in the main, has decided to use his accumulated knowledge to assist other referees instead of refereeing an actual game. The higher up the refereeing ladder we go the more we are assessed. That being the case, I was seldom the recipient of an assessor's comments but I do remember the several occasions when an assessor paid me a visit.

The first time I was assessed was the second game I reffed for London Society. He turned up late and then came up to me at half-time, told me he was an assessor and what he had so far found wrong with my refereeing! After the game he walked back with me towards the changing rooms and told me that I had improved a little during the second half; climbed into his car and drove away. In the bar afterwards, both captains told me that they much more enjoyed the first half than the second half when I appeared to be trying to ingratiate myself with the assessor and stopped the flow of the game as a consequence. So that was a first lesson learned. Always ignore the assessor if you become aware of one, during the game. We are there for the players and their good opinion of the way we referee is worth far more than pleasing an assessor (unless you want to be promoted!).

I was unaware of my second assessor a few weeks later as there was more than one spectator on the touch line. It was a game that the visitors lost because of the stupidity of their captain. Rightly or wrongly, he disagreed with several of my decisions and then convinced his side that I was not only totally incompetent, but also completely biased against his team. The consequence was that all his players were watching me and not their opponents. Frankly, if you look hard enough for bias and mistakes you will find them, especially when you regard your own team's misdemeanours through rose-coloured spectacles. After the game, two people came up to me simultaneously. The first was the captain of the visiting and losing side saying that I was the worst referee he had ever had the misfortune to meet. (I doubt if he was impressed when I called him over towards the end of the game and asked him to point out his vice captain. On asking me why, I told him that if I heard another word of criticism of my decisions from him, I would send him off so I needed to know in advance who would take over the captaincy. Whilst I did not get another peep out of him on the field, he had his say immediately after the game!) In my other ear, a man said, 'I am a London Society assessor and I was watching you this afternoon. How did you think it went?'

I replied, 'Well you heard what the visiting captain thought!'

In a very loud and penetrating voice, my assessor said, 'Don't take any notice of him. That was the comment of a poor losing captain!' He went on to tell me that I had had a reasonable game and spent some time with me pointing out where I could improve. It is not very pleasant being heavily criticised in the way I had been subjected to by the visiting captain and I was most grateful to have an independent voice assuring me that I was nowhere near as bad as had been made out.

During my years with London Society, we had two different types of club assessment of our refereeing. Initially, only the home club received a card that asked for an assessment of the referee's overall performance from A – Excellent, to E – Poor. Over a season, this gave a reflection on how well or otherwise clubs viewed their referees. Of course, it would be unrealistic to think that home wins were marked slightly more leniently than away wins.

One senior referee underlined this point when he wound up his talk on the art of refereeing at the beginning of the season with the words, 'And may all your games be home wins!'

The system was not perfect. One school sent in a card after the game officiated by an England International panel referee with an E grade. The referee understandably was not amused, nor was the London Society chairman, who wrote to the school and advised them that as the Society's most experienced referee was obviously not good enough for their school, there was no point in sending any other Society referees to take their games. The headmaster was on the phone immediately apologising and advising the Society that the master in charge of rugby had been dismissed from this position and that the school captain would re-mark the card – with an A!

On another occasion, a referee who had consistently received A and B grades all season suddenly received an E grade. The list secretary was intrigued by this and phoned the club contact to find out why he had graded this referee with an E grade, thinking there must be some mistake. 'Because there wasn't an F on the card' came the reply.

Art and Style

BRIAN MOORE

The former England hooker tells how referees are best approached. From *Beware of the Dog: Rugby's Hard Man Tells All* (2010).

INFLUENCING REFEREES IS an art and each player has his own style. Sean Fitzpatrick and George Gregan, from the All Blacks and the Wallabies respectively, were never short of helpful observations. Martin Johnson was the English equivalent, and I tried my best, sometimes successfully. As with many allegations about me, the claim that I constantly spoke to referees is not true. It may have seemed like that, but I was well aware that no referee would tolerate constant talking; and more importantly, it would not have worked because a referee would eventually have become impervious to anything I said, whether or not it had merit.

I used to pose questions such as 'How did their flanker get in that position?' The posing of the question forced the referee to consider the point, and he would look out for it thereafter. Most referees did not mind a comment that was made in a light-hearted manner. In one game, the referee called me to one side and told me to stop trying to referee the game. He did not take offence when I replied that one of us had to do this, and as he hadn't seemed that interested ...

Noises On

JEFF PROBYN AND BARRY NEWCOMBE

Playing against the All Blacks, England prop Jeff Probyn is less worried by
his front row opponent than by the way the New Zealanders manipulate the
referee. From *Upfront: The Jeff Probyn Story* (1993).

I TOOK MORE NOTICE of the noise the All Blacks made. Everything which
happened brought this chorus of noise – 'Look, ref, he's holding the ball', or
'Look, ref, he's off-side', and so on. All the time they were telling the referee,
Jim Fleming of Scotland in this case, how the game should be played and
there is no doubt this has an effect on the referee. Referees are intimidated by
the great New Zealand name. You can see it is part of their tactics – and sides
which are coached by New Zealanders do the same. Northampton are great
talkers and so are London Irish. Both have New Zealand coaches and I am
sure New Zealanders use the referee as part of the game, drawing his attention
to things that happen to them, not to the things they do. They cast doubt in a
referee's mind about an event even if it looks alright. The referee may not react
to that incident but he could react next time. It also puts doubt in your mind
as a player. You could be running and hear 'Ref, knock on, knock on' and that
could slow you down. You half check, thinking the referee might blow. Good
referees are not affected by it but the tactic exists. When you have the ball you
do not expect the amount of noise which comes at you. Nobody had warned
us but other teams will develop it if they believe it will work for them.

An Unforgiving Place

NICK BISHOP AND ALUN CARTER

Corris Thomas referees a dreaded Wednesday night Pontypool game.
From *The Good, The Bad and The Ugly: The Rise and Fall of Pontypool RFC* (2013).

࣭

IT WAS AN unforgiving place to be, but I always felt it was worse on those Wednesday nights than it was on Saturday afternoons. There was a palpable difference in the atmosphere. Eddie Butler once told me he didn't think Pontypool always had the extra edge they needed for those crunch weekend games.

I remember a game between Pontypool and Bridgend on one of those Wednesday nights. Pontypool were in total control up front, but it was still a close game coming into the final minutes; Pontypool were leading 13–8, I think. They had a line-out on the final play of the game, only a few metres from the Bridgend line. I was ready to blow the whistle the next time the ball went dead.

Somehow Bridgend won the line-out. Chris Williams spun it out to JPR in the shadow of his own posts. Somehow JPR worked his way upfield and somehow the ball ended up in the hands of the Bridgend prop Meredydd James, who scored in between the posts. I remember the look on Meredydd's face quite clearly; he looked like the boy who'd just escaped from the sweet shop with some penny blackjacks! So now it was 13–12, with an easy conversion to come, and I was looking over my shoulder with some concern. I was a good fifty metres away from the tunnel!

The goal was duly converted and I blew the whistle and ran for my life. Pooler supporters were flooding onto the field, screaming in my face; I could see the wild eyes and the contorted mouths spewing out the abuse. I tried to ignore it, but then one of them grabbed hold of me, and I thought, 'Oh, Jesus… what do I do now? Say "Un-hand me, sir" or "I'm a chartered accountant"'…No. That wouldn't work.

Salvation, when it came, arrived from an unexpected quarter. Suddenly Bobby Windsor was alongside me, throwing the 'supporter' who had manhandled me to the ground. His arm moved around my shoulder and I can still remember the strength of his grip as he towed me along: 'You 'ad a bloody good game, you b*****d!' he said out of the corner of his mouth as he marched me all the way down to the tunnel, with the supporters now forming a respectful cordon around the both of us.

I cannot describe how grateful I was for his actions at that moment, and I've never forgotten the impression. Moments like that stay with you for a lifetime. But it was typical of the Pontypool volte-face – ruthless and brutal on the field but entirely social and fair-minded off it. Even a man as utterly implacable and cruel as Bobby had that sense of social conscience – I guess that's the phrase – once the game had ended.

'To the Whistle'

'ALFRED JINGLE'

Although written well over a hundred years ago, this poem shows that attitudes towards the referee have not changed very much. From *Rugby Rhymes, Rough and Ready* (1893).

Blow on, old man, blow on,
Like any bo's'un bold,
Blow on!
It's true I feel a trifle sold—
I gave the man his five yards good,
Five yards and more from where I stood;
But there – I don't want to be rude,
Don't mind what *I* say!
You blow on!

Blow on, old man, blow on!
Yes, here we are again!
Blow on!
And what's up now you'll p'r'ps explain.
What – *that* 'picked out'? Why, dash it all,
That wasn't any kind of maul,

I don't see that you've any call
To interfere,
Be blowed!
[*And it* is *blowed!*]

6

BEYOND THE TOUCHLINE

A Long Memory

W. ROWE HARDING

The vibrant personality of a Welsh crowd is depicted by Harding
who played seventeen times for Wales in the 1920s.
From *Rugby Reminiscences and Opinions* (1929).

～

RUGBY IN WALES is a democratic game, and the crowd is no respecter of persons. The fact that one plays rugby is a sufficient introduction to every Welsh rugby follower, and consequently one has an embarrassingly large number of friends of all kinds, who insist upon talking rugby when they meet one. After one international match at Swansea I was hailed by a complete stranger who said, 'Hallo, Rowe boy, I suppose you remember me?' I had to confess that I did not. 'Don't you remember a photograph in the papers of you coming off the field after the Irish match at Swansea, and two fellows patting you on the back? That was me and my mate.' If a rugby player's Christian name is Joe, he is known to the crowd as Joe, be he butcher, miner, lawyer, or preacher. There is one exception, a doctor is always referred to as 'Doctor', whether he be a doctor of medicine, music, or philosophy. Of course, if one plays a bad game, he will be called other names, all expressions of ridicule, hatred and contempt, comparing him to his more remote maternal ancestor, to a feminine apple vendor of advanced years, and to all slow-footed and clumsy animals of a lower order than man. A Welsh crowd has a long memory and never forgets an offence against its susceptibilities. Years ago I played for Llanelly and then, so they say at Llanelly, deserted to Swansea. Ever since I have been an object of derision and contempt, whenever I have appeared on the classic slopes of Stradey. Even the smallest child is taught to boo when my name is mentioned. Similarly, whenever Jack Wetter's bald pate was seen emerging from the pavilion at Swansea, the crowd greeted him with shouts of 'Play the game, Wetter.' I have never been able to discover why Wetter should be singled out for obloquy, but doubtless some time in the distant past he fell foul of the crowd, and the tradition has been handed on and still persists. Even now, when he appears at St Helen's in the capacity of a referee, he is exhorted to 'Play the game.'

Every club has among its spectators supporters who, by reason of their loyalty, lung power, or personal eccentricity, have become well known to the crowd. Llanelly had for years as camp follower a well-known character called 'Tosh' Evans, who followed the team about wherever they went, and on Derby days, as when Swansea played Llanelly, conducted the inevitable preliminaries, ran on the field, swarmed up a goal-post and deposited a saucepan, the Llanelly emblem, on the top. At half-time he amused the crowd with an eccentric dance which he performed in the middle of the field, juggling the while with his hat and a walking-stick. Swansea rejoices in the vociferous support of Mr Derricott, who has followed Swansea Rugby, man and boy, for nearly fifty years. He is a powerful man, with a booming fog-horn voice, and he is always attired in white moleskin trousers, and every Saturday when Swansea play at St Helen's, whether the crowd numbers twenty thousand or a mere handful of people, Derricott's deep voice booms across the field at intervals, like a minute gun at sea: 'Play up, the whites!' It is a voice which has been heard by generations of rugby players and spectators at St Helen's, and I for one have derived consolation and encouragement from it when things have been going badly for the side.

❧

They Also Serve Who Only Stand and Watch

CHRIS LAIDLAW

The most famous New Zealand spectator, Little Eric of Berhampore, was a
cartoon character drawn by A. S. Paterson. Eric appeared in the Wellington
Dominion Post for twenty-five years or so from the 1920s. Chris Laidlaw won
twenty caps as a scrum-half for New Zealand and went on to have a career in
politics, public service and broadcasting. From *Mud in Your Eye* (1973).

I T I S A strange thing that individually, rugby enthusiasts tend to be the most
reasonable of people, yet collectively they are all too often merciless. The
psychology of mass behaviour of course reveals a tendency on the part of large
groups towards belligerence. Security is provided by numbers and the nice
average chap who wouldn't dream of shouting or doing anything untoward
if he were all alone up there on the bank will often let himself be completely
carried away when surrounded by like minds. Take that most celebrated hero
of New Zealand spectators, Little Eric of Berhampore. From Monday to
Friday Little Eric is a mouse. He is everywhere, unnoticed, grey of suit, white
of shirt, voice never raised, let alone heard. He absorbs orders and criticism
as naturally as his daily bread. On Saturday he makes his way calmly and
discreetly to Athletic Park and takes up his customary station on the western
bank without a murmur. Then upon the first blast of the whistle he becomes a
lion. For eighty minutes with a moment to catch his breath after forty of them,
Little Eric rules the park with his fiery condemnation of the 'other' team and
his cries of agonised incitement to his own team who can do no wrong. He
above all knows and reveals the weakness of the smartest of referees. When
the match is over his indignation must be gradually sluiced away with rapid
glasses of beer, and during the ensuing hours his voice gradually loses its
authority, his judgements become less certain and uncompromising. By the
time he reaches home he is again a mouse, a tired and deflated one. Terry
McLean thinks that Little Eric of Berhampore is dead and gone. I don't, he is
still there every week and just as schizophrenic.

A Childhood Prophecy

ROBERT COLLIS

Collis (1900–75), a paediatrician, has been called the Irish Schindler for his work in caring for children after the liberation of Bergen-Belsen. This extract from *The Silver Fleece* (1936) starts with his introduction to rugby.

❧

THE TEACHING AT Aravon in those days may have been unusual, but I shall always be glad I went to the school for one reason – the 'rugger'. Unlike many English preparatory schools that play 'soccer', Aravon specialised in rugby football. It was there at the age of nine that I was first introduced to the great game, in playing which I have lived more truly, I think, than at any other time in my life. I can still remember vividly my first game. I can visualise the black jersey with the yellow Maltese cross on the breast and recall its smell as I slipped it over my head. Then there is a gap in the picture till I am standing on the ground by the touch-line watching the junior game. It is an autumn day, the wind blowing from the west out of the glens of Wicklow, moist and soft and full of the smell of wet leaves. The sky is cloudy. The ground is a somewhat sloping field at the foot of Bray Head. A master explains the principles of the game to me, and with this scant instruction I am sent out to play. Immediately I step into my element as if born to the game. Soon the ball is in my hands and I am running with it. When the game is over the master comes up to me and tells me that some day I shall become an International and play for Ireland. Then and there I am promoted to the senior game.

I never forgot this moment, and when, fifteen years later, the prophecy came true and I got my Irish cap, my first action was to wire the news to the little old man. Since then he has told the story over and over again in the local golf club to anyone who will listen.

By my second year at the school I was playing for the Fifteen. Matches with other schools became a great thrill as time went on, lighting up the day before and the morning of the match with the excitement of anticipation. There was the train journey, sometimes into Dublin, the meeting with the other team, the glory of the game, and the ecstasy of eating a big tea afterwards. I think few people realise the immense pleasure growing boys obtain from filling themselves up with food. It is the only time in life when the actual capacity of the stomach is the sole legitimate limit.

More exciting than these contests of our own, more important than any other event in the year, were the Internationals at Lansdowne Road, to which we were always allowed to go. We may have known more about the Wars of the Roses and the battle of Agincourt than about the Four Masters and the Siege of Limerick, but on these occasions there was no question upon which side we were. All our loyalty, and a very passionate one it was too, went out to the men in green jerseys. They were our gods – particularly Dickie Lloyd, McIvor, and old bald-headed Hamlet. Dickie Lloyd always retrieved the Irish fortunes when all seemed lost, by some miraculous kick; McIvor could run like a deer; Hamlet, who appeared a great age to us, seemed to be able to survive frightful mauls which left lesser stalwarts prostrate on the field.

The great match between England and Ireland, about 1911, when Ireland won by one try to *nil*, remains in the minds of many the greatest match of all time. The story of the match is commonplace enough. Ireland scored off a forward rush just after half-time, and then held out against a most determined English attack till the whistle blew. Such a description, however, in no way represents what happened in reality that early spring afternoon. Thirty thousand people forgot who they were, dropped their masks and became a mob, a herd, with but one will. Unionists and Nationalists, Ulstermen and Munstermen, Catholics and Protestants, and unathletic intellectuals who had been brought protesting by their families, all became affected alike. All yelled 'IRELAND!' till their throats only emitted a croak. When Ireland scored we all went mad. We stood up and yelled and yelled and yelled; a man from the West near us lost his hat – threw it away; we roared in triumph, all restraint gone. During the desperate English counter-attack towards the end the excitement rose higher; the cheering rolled backwards and forwards from one side of the field to the other in waves, sometimes sinking almost to a sob when our men seemed about to be overcome. At last the whistle blew for 'time'. The tension broke, and with one accord the crowd rushed on to the ground to carry off victor and vanquished alike, shoulder high.

The Turning Point

PHIL VICKERY WITH ALISON KERVIN

After working his way up through junior rugby, the England prop forward, aged nineteen, joins Gloucester, but feels homesick and out of place. From The Raging Bull: The Autobiography of the English Rugby Legend (2010).

❧

THE TURNING POINT for me and Gloucester, and the moment when I started to enjoy playing rugby rather than disliking everything about my new life, was when I realised, truly realised, what a big deal rugby was for the locals, and what a huge passion people had for the sport in the area. I think when I first got there I had my head down and was training and working hard, trying to cope in an alien environment which I didn't think suited me, but when I lifted my head, looked around and saw that the town was full of rugby nuts who really wanted the team to win, I started to come round a bit and to think that this might actually be a good place to play rugby.

Gloucester is a relatively small town, despite my initial view that it was a big city, and it comes alive on match days. Rugby is a big part of people's lives and supporters know the names of the players, and understand the sport inside out and back to front. They can debate all the finer points of tactics and team play with you, and they know exactly who they think should be in the team, and who they feel, very strongly, should not be in the team.

I remember walking into a pub in Gloucester and everyone turning round to look at me. Their eyes followed me as I walked through to the bar. When I got there, the barman stuck his hand out and shook mine and welcomed me, and the locals wouldn't let me buy a drink. They really enjoyed being able to talk about rugby to someone in the team, and chat about how I thought Gloucester would get on that season.

I loved the people of Gloucester because I realised they were *my* people. Like those who I'd grown up with back in Bude, they were decent, hard-working guys who enjoyed their rugby and a few pints on a Saturday night. Most of them watched Gloucester play at the weekend but were also involved in the small clubs in the area – clubs that were exactly like Bude. I realised I was among good people who I could relate to and wanted to do well for. They were builders, carpenters, butchers, farmers – the sort of people for whom tickets weren't cheap, and who were making a big sacrifice to support the team. I felt I wanted to do well for them.

The supporters react with passion whenever Gloucester play, especially if the opponents are rivals and neighbours, like Bath or Bristol. If you do well, they adore you; if you don't play well for their beloved Gloucester side, heaven help you. In the week leading up to a match the excitement in the town rises to fever pitch. It's a challenge, a mighty challenge, and I felt suddenly very up for that challenge.

My first game for Gloucester was against Bath. In the Bath team at the time were players like Dave Hilton, John Mallett and Steve Ojomoh. These were guys I had seen on television who were now going to be playing against me. It was a second-team game, but we still had 6,000 people there to watch, which was roughly six times as many people as I'd played in front of before.

I found that I loved the banter and the fierce support of the guys in the infamous Shed. I enjoyed meeting the supporters afterwards and feeling part of something that mattered to people. The more my attitude changed, and I started enjoying rugby and working hard at it, the more I enjoyed being in Gloucester. Suddenly the dark days were behind me and I was starting to really enjoy my rugby . . . and my life.

The other great memory that stands out for me about Gloucester is of the number of children involved in the club. There were always children around, involved in the youth section, supporting the players, hunting for autographs. It gave the club a really nice feel.

I wanted to play well and to get into the first team. There was still a lot of home-grown talent playing at Gloucester, so if I was going to work my way into the team, and into the affections of the supporters, I needed to be good. I realised that I'd been drifting and not getting really stuck into training. I needed to work very hard to get myself noticed by Richard Hill and be given a chance in the main side. Once I started putting the hours in, training hard, and embracing the lifestyle, I started to love the place, the people and the rugby club even more.

Captain's Poker

STEPHEN GAUGE

Having risen to the dizzy heights of fourth-team captain, the author has to
attend selection meetings with the other team captains. From *My Life as a
Hooker: When a Middle-Aged Bloke Discovered Rugby* (2012).

❧

AT THE SELECTION meeting with the other team captains and club coaches,
I had to be very careful how I described my chances of getting a side
out at the weekend, and play my cards very close to my chest. On Tuesday
evenings in the club's committee room a five-day-long game of 'Captains'
Hold 'em Poker' begins. The rules are as follows:

First the club manager deals out cards with the players' names on to each
of the captains. Unlike normal poker he deals the first fifteen to the first-team
captain, the second fifteen to the second-team captain and so on. The fourth-
team captain gets whatever cards are left at the end. The first-team captain will
then 'see' players in the other sides that he likes the look of and take them. He
may possibly 'discard' a few of his own cards of players he knows are injured,
working or likely to be arrested for being drunk and disorderly on the Friday
night. Players are swapped and shuffled around until one team has less than
ten players. That team then 'folds', i.e. cancels its game, and the other captains
then scrabble around to grab the players for their own team.

The only way to succeed at Captains' Poker from the fourth-team seat is
to have approximately ten players on the table, who are known to be worse
than useless. All the other captains then feel able to ignore these. Meanwhile
you need to have another stack of players up your sleeve that no one else
knows about, who have declared their availability only to you. You then need
to smuggle them into the clubhouse, if necessary wearing sunglasses and a
false beard, about five minutes before the kick-off.

If you don't have any other players up your sleeve, then you need to pull
off a serious 'bluff'. This is to convince not just the other captains, but also the
club administrators, that you will still somehow manage to get a side out and
honour the fixture. You also need to convince the very few players that have
ended up in your side that it will be worth their while turning up. If they get a
sniff of the possibility that you might be short of numbers and they will either

end up playing in three positions simultaneously or the game as a whole will be scrapped, then they may go and find something better to do with their Saturday afternoon.

In the later rounds of the game a new pack of player cards are introduced one by one over the next few days, any time up to about half an hour before the kick-off, as a few disorganised club members and friends of members turn up looking for a game. Captains then compete to lure the new players into their sides by offering preferred playing positions, promises of post-match alcohol and possible sexual favours. During this phase of the game, teams with away fixtures are at a distinct disadvantage as they will need to be on the road and out of the poker game an hour or so earlier than anyone else.

In a further complication, you have to remember that other clubs will also be playing their own version of Captains' Poker and every now and again one of your opponents' sides will cry off their game as they run out of players. This leads to another unseemly scramble to snaffle up the players left kicking their heels before they are dragged off to IKEA by their wives and girlfriends.

Just to confuse matters further, the playing cards have minds of their own and will occasionally decide that they are no longer available to play for the captain to whom they have been dealt, having developed a mysterious injury, work commitment or terminal hangover.

And so I have as fourth-team captain at various points in my career started a game with fifteen keen beans on the pitch and a further fifteen on the touchline, changed, warmed up and stretched off, eager to get on. On other days I have been at an away fixture hiding in a changing room minutes before the scheduled kick-off with barely ten or eleven players, most of whom can only manage twenty minutes of a game at best before collapsing from exhaustion.

However, whatever hand I had been dealt, I made it a point of principle never to turn away a potential player, and never to cry off a fixture. Away matches were always the hardest to recruit players for but if the worst came to the worst, I would take whatever number of players I had with me and try and make the best of a bad job.

Court of No Appeal

BRIAN MOORE

Behind the scenes on the 1990 England tour of Argentina,
Beware of the Dog: Rugby's Hard Man Tells All (2010) shows the
workings of the 'players' revolutionary court' where punishments are handed
out for purported offences. A hooker, Brian Moore played sixty-four times for
England and six times for the British and Irish Lions.

AN IMPORTANT MATTER required attention before we could plan for the tour's first court session: we needed a new judge. Paul Rendall had always filled this role, hence his nickname of 'Judge'. In his place we appointed the West Midlands policeman and Moseley prop, Mark Linnet.

It was traditional at the end of a tour for there to be a players' revolutionary court. This turned the tables on the court officials who had handed out punishments during the previous sittings. Linnet's punishment was that he had to wear, beneath his formal dress of tour blazer, tie and trousers, a lurid bikini that was several sizes too small for his ample figure. On a limited number of occasions, whenever a certain word was shouted out, he had to perform a striptease wherever he was at the time. The first call came in an airport concourse, but after the second, which came just after the security scanners, it was decided that it should be withdrawn on the grounds that he was enjoying it too much.

In a normal tour court, a number of officials were required. I was chief prosecutor, assorted second-row players were made court enforcers, and the court sneak, Mr X, went to the eminently qualified Jon Olver, known to all as Vermin. Mr X's role was to agitate for information on which we could base a variety of charges. He was frequently called upon to give evidence, but due to the clandestine nature of his activities, he did this disguised in a hat and dark glasses. As a court official, his testimony was irrefutable and he sent many players to their doom.

Mickey Skinner provided two of the tour's best stories. Having been late for training again, he and three other players were made to run back to the hotel after training, about four miles. Roger Uttley, the coach who imposed this penalty, sportingly did the run with them, but as Roger was super-fit this gesture did not impress the miscreants, especially as we encouraged them warmly whilst getting on the coach. Roger set off bounding down the street, followed less swiftly by three of the players with Skinner bringing up the rear. When he considered the other runners were out of sight, Skinner stopped and got in a taxi. We saw this from the bus and tried to alert Roger to it but failed because of the traffic noise.

For the rest of the journey, Skinner waved from the cab, which followed our coach as we crawled through traffic. As we neared the hotel we saw Roger standing atop the entrance to the hotel, which resembled the police patrol positions on the side of motorways. The taxi overtook us and we stopped in waiting traffic. As we watched, the taxi, now seemingly unoccupied, edged slowly up the ramp towards Roger, stopping a couple of times. It reached the apex and then did the same on its way down the other side and then drove off round the corner of the hotel and out of sight. During this journey, Skinner had lain on the floor in the back of the taxi repeatedly asking if a tall man who looked like Mr Potato Head was still standing there. When he received the answer 'yes', he had told the cabbie to drive a bit further. As we got off the bus, we saw Skinner walk back round the corner and approach Roger and say, 'Rog, have you got any money for the cab?'

Skinner's lack of punctuality eventually got him a warning that serious measures would meet any further lateness. We all gleefully registered his absence at the start of one morning meeting a few days later. He did not appear and we left for training without him, each of us making suggestions as to what punishment would be given. Half an hour into training, Skinner appeared, accompanied by our diminutive liaison officer, whose first name was 'Fafa'. In broken English, Fafa proceeded to tell us about Skinner apprehending a would-be burglar caught in our team room. I had my doubts as soon as Fafa started to describe how Skinner had wrestled the man to the floor and heroically summoned the hotel security staff. However, the story was accepted by the management and players, and training resumed. It was not until we were on the plane home that Skinner confirmed what I had suspected, that this was a lie concocted to avoid the serious trouble he knew he was in when he overslept because of a heavy night.

∽

Cured by Kowhai

GEORGE NEPIA AND TERRY McLEAN

In I, George Nepia *(2002), the legendary All Blacks full-back (1924–30) tells how he suffered an injury that failed to heal and threatened his career in its early stages.*

THE POINT OF greatest interest to me was the injury I suffered in tackling Neil McGregor too late in the game for any replacement to be necessary. His elbow struck my thigh and burst a blood vessel. The medical men told me it was a haematoma and said there was nothing to worry about. They might have been right – but I was conscious of the fact that the left leg had stiffened immediately after the collision and that I could not walk properly on it.

Norman McKenzie was as worried as I. He brought me back from Invercargill to Napier for treatment by a masseur, Hildebrandt, who had a reputation as one of the best physiotherapists in the country. While under this treatment, which went on for a fortnight, I played, as full-back, in a shield challenge made by Canterbury and which we won by 24 to 18, but I could not play against Southland three days later in a match forever famous because during it the referee, Mr Bill Meredith, of Auckland, told W. E. Hazlett, the nineteen-year-old forward from Southland, 'Now then, Hazlett, you leave *Mr* Brownlie alone!'

It was not, in fact, for another fortnight that I could again play. Meanwhile these were important days. Hildebrandt worked on me twice daily for a fortnight without real improvement. He even tried Turkish baths with the idea of heating my whole body so that the bruise would come out. Finally, he said: 'George, I don't know what to do. I have tried everything. Nothing has happened. I'll have to call in a doctor.'

In came the doctor. He examined the leg very carefully. 'I will have to operate,' he said. 'The blood has congealed. If it is not taken away you could get blood-poisoning.' 'No knife for me,' I said flatly. 'I'm off.'

I had already been told by Lui Paewai's mother that she would treat me. Kowhai, she said. The bark of the Kowhai. That is what you need. She met me at the train at Dannevirke and we drove to the farm at Tahoraiti, a few miles out. There, in a stand of bush there were hundreds of kowhai trees. Mrs Paewai told me what I must do. Only the bark facing the rays of the sun was to be taken from the trees. Then we started. Not until we had filled two big sacks with bark did we stop. Later, I was told to cut the strips into short lengths of about a foot and to hammer each length until it was bruised. Next the strips were put into a copper full of water and for two or three hours I kept the water at the boil until it had turned a dark tan in colour. This was ladled into a bath and as soon as the temperature was right I stripped off and lay full length. A full hour I stayed there before Mrs Paewai returned to inspect the leg. By now, it was discoloured in many places. When she went out of the room, I heard a bottle break. When she came back, she made me hold my leg out of the water. In two of her fingers, she held a smallish piece of glass and with this she started to dab my thigh, cutting little nicks all around the leg from the knee up.

More of the hot bark water was added. I must remain in the bath, Mrs Paewai said, for another hour.

I slept. When I woke, the water had turned a deep dark shade of brown. The colour seemed to be coming to the surface from my leg. I called out to Mrs Paewai. As she came in, I lifted my leg. From out of all the little nicks there was oozing dark blood. She was jubilant. She cried out in Maori, again and again, 'Kua pai tou waewae' (your leg is better).

You will have no more worry, she said. In a week's time, you will be playing. There will be no more trouble. What a contrast, I thought. A Pakeha doctor had told me I would not play again during the season. The injury is too serious, he said. A Maori woman, using Maori treatment had cured me. Play soon, she said.

Back in Napier, I showed the leg to Mr McKenzie and to Hildebrandt. Only here and there could you find trace of the nicks. The majority were healed. Mr McKenzie was pleased. Hildebrandt was ecstatic. 'It is a miracle,' he said. 'I did not tell you, but I knew your leg was in a bad way. A very bad way. I doubt that an operation would have helped. I was almost certain your playing career was finished.'

❧

Don't Swear!

H. B. T. WAKELAM

In *The Mike and Me* (1938), the first man to broadcast rugby live describes
the nervous early days. St Dunstan's was a charity set up during the First World
War to train blinded servicemen for employment.
It still exists today as Blind Veterans UK.

❧

ONE AFTERNOON I was sitting at my table, working out some details of a
tender, when my telephone rang.

An unknown voice at the other end then asked me if I was the same
Wakelam who had played rugger for the Harlequins, and, upon my saying
'Yes,' went on to inform me that the owner of it was an official of the British
Broadcasting Corporation, who would much like to see me at once on an
urgent matter.

Turning up at the arranged meeting-place, I was welcomed by Lance
Sieveking, the gentleman in question, who thereupon explained to me the
reason for his call. Briefly, it was this. Since the BBC in January 1927 had
become a national institution, its scope had become considerably wider,
and it had been decided to follow a recent American innovation, and to put
out running commentaries on important sporting events. It was proposed
that a start should be made with the rugby international at Twickenham,
between England and Wales, on 15 January, and would I be prepared to
undergo there and then a studio microphone test in order to see if my voice
was suitable, and then, should such prove to be the case, to take part in an
actual field trial to be held the next day on the Guy's Hospital Ground at
Honor Oak Park? On the principle of 'try anything once' and also with the
confirmed conviction that if an American could do it I could, I agreed, and
duly passed the 'mike' test.

. . . After it was over, Sieveking came up to me, and asked me if I would
have a shot at doing the match as proposed. I agreed, subject, of course, to
suitable financial remuneration, a point upon which both of us very naturally
were quite at sea. That, however, was put aside for the moment, and we set out
straightaway for Twickenham to examine the selection position and to study
the arrangements.

Arriving at Twickenham, Sieveking and I were met by Commander Cooper, an old and valued friend of mine, and together we examined our perch, which was a somewhat rickety-looking hut mounted on a scaffold platform at the end of the then single-decker West Stand, in the south-west corner. Here the engineers were hard at work wiring up and installing the microphones, and we for our own part worked out in detail our proposed plan of campaign. Here the first squared plan of the field came into being, the facsimile of which so often nowadays is printed for the benefit of listeners in the *Radio Times*, and here was put up a notice for our own particular benefit, a notice which, printed in large red letters, was constantly to remind me of my whereabouts, for it said 'DON'T SWEAR' (not that I any more than the rest of my fellow-men am addicted to the use of strong language, but sometimes, watching rugger, one is apt to get carried away!). The order of seating was also decided upon, and Sieveking finally was struck with a most brilliant idea, which was to prove of the utmost worth to me on the day. He decided to get hold of a St Dunstan's man who, before his terrible misfortune, had been a keen rugger follower, and to invite him to sit just in front of the open window of the box so that I could talk as if explaining the game directly to him, and so perhaps lose some of my very natural stage-fright. Having fixed these and other small details, we returned to town, and duly reassembled on the site an hour or so before the game on the fateful day. Then I learnt that it had been decided that Charles Lapworth should be my 'No. 2', or, as someone immediately and appropriately remarked, my 'Dr Watson'. In many ways he was very well suited to his job, for he was the personification of cool and calm collectedness, though his knowledge of the actual game itself was rather limited. In fact, the only football he really knew at all was the American game, as one of his remarks was to prove.

With feelings rather similar to those which I imagine must run through the mind of a prisoner about to make the 'eight o'clock walk', I mounted the ladder on to the scaffold, there to become the butt of many of my more light-hearted and evil-minded friends, who took the opportunity to gather below on the ground and to pass a lot of rude and scathing remarks at my expense. However, the arrival of several Press photographers, as well as some of the BBC officials, soon took my mind off such trivialities, and it did not seem very long before we were planted in position in the box, myself on the right, Lapworth in the middle, and Sieveking, in charge of the party, next to the door. Immediately in front was the St Dunstan's man, and the stage was set.

Ten minutes before the kick-off, we came on the air, Sieveking first to give the atmosphere, reading out the now familiar copyright notice and doing the introductions, and then a somewhat shy and diffident me, to give out the details of the game and the names of those taking part in it. On the stroke of the appointed time, the match was started, and we were off. Straightaway I forgot all my nervousness and stage-fright, all my previously and arduously collected phrases, and all the, as I thought, snappy and pithy expressions which I had anxiously culled from the leading sporting writers of the day. I was so wrapped up in following the flight and fortunes of that ball, and so desperately keen to keep my St Dunstan's man fully informed, that I raced away like a maniac, and then and there, I think, got into the habit (which I still maintain is essential) of being just a fraction of a second ahead of the actual game. By that I mean the necessity of starting to speak of a man as passing just as he is shaping to pass, a poor description and example to illustrate my point, but nevertheless a correct one, for it is actually the truth.

Out of the corner of my eye I saw Lapworth and Sieveking looking at me with an air of amazement so pronounced that I almost stopped and asked them what was the matter, but luckily I carried on, as I had been told to do, in face of everything, to be informed at the end that they were only wondering when I was going to blow up!

My memories of the actual game itself that day are, I am afraid, very vague indeed, in fact I do not believe when it was over that I could recall one single football incident, though I do remember some of the gap-filling remarks which are, of course, essential when play is temporarily held up for this or that reason.

Once Lapworth, doing a hero's work in all conscience, said to me in one of these pauses, 'Do they always play with an oval ball?', a remark which may to any rugger player appear ludicrous, but it reminded me that many of my audience were not familiar with the game, and so helped me to keep away from being too technical (a most serious fault). Again, he said, after one of the Englishmen had been hurt, and had had to leave the field, 'Who will they send on instead?' another apparent bloomer, but a chance for me to fill in by saying that the practice of replacements had not so far (and I sincerely hope never will) become part of the rugby football creed. And so, with Lapworth's calm voice occasionally bringing me back to earth, and tempering my Celtic fervour, with Sieveking's commanding hand sometimes waving me back when I crowded on to the mike and so was in danger of blasting, and with the 'Don't swear' notice ever before my eyes, I got somehow to half-time, and a welcome breathing-space, filled in by atmosphere from the outside mike, and a few more remarks by Sieveking.

Hereabouts I am popularly supposed to have remarked, *sotto voce* (which of course makes no difference), 'What about having a drink?' but if such was the case, I have no recollection of it, and prefer to treat it as a *canard*.

In five minutes we were off again, and though towards the end I do recall becoming rather breathless and hoarse, my general memory of the second half is as blank as that of the first.

I do, however, distinctly remember an enormous feeling of relief at 'no side', a feeling which I still have today, after ten solid years of it. It is, I suppose, more of a reaction than a relief, but anyway it is a very pleasant sensation of something accomplished, something done.

7

GIVING IT EVERYTHING

The War Game

TONY COLLINS

Scotland are playing England in Edinburgh. It is March 1914 and the next
Calcutta Cup game will not take place till 1920. In *A Social History of English
Rugby Union* (2009), Tony Collins tells what happens to some of the
players in the intervening years.

❧

IT WAS A clear, crisp Edinburgh afternoon in early spring. Blustery wind had
dried away the rain that had swept over the city earlier, leaving a sharp bite
of anticipation in the air. It was Calcutta Cup day and England were in town.
As the crowd made its way to Scotland's Inverleith ground in the northern
suburbs of the city, the streets echoed to the talk of England's unbeaten run of
two seasons, of the brilliance of its captain Ronald Poulton-Palmer, and of the
chances of the underdog Scots that afternoon. It was March 1914.

The match was a classic. In the first half the Scots failed to take full
advantage of the wind blowing behind them but, realising that a kicking game
was impossible, the English backs relied on a passing game. For once it was
not Poulton-Palmer who carved up the opposition with slashing runs but his
centre partner 'Bungy' Watson. However, it was the Scots who took the lead
midway through the first half when Scottish forward Fred Turner got a pass
out to winger John Will who touched down with defenders still hanging on
to him. But English pressure told and just before half-time Watson beat two
defenders and threw an inside pass to his winger Cyril Lowe who tied the
game up at three-all.

Scottish hopes of an upset rose even higher when their forwards over-ran
the English pack a minute into the second half and Turner again laid on the
final pass for debutant James Huggan to go over in the corner. This seemed to
bring out the steel in the English: Watson and Poulton-Palmer took charge.
Watson again opened the Scots' defence to send Lowe in for his second try,

which Harrison converted to put England ahead for the first time. A passing movement involving four players put Lowe in for his hat-trick in the corner, which Harrison magnificently converted from the touch-line. Watson then stepped through a clutch of defenders to send Poulton-Palmer over by the posts, which Harrison inexplicably failed to convert.

Twenty minutes to go and England were ahead 16–6. The Calcutta Cup and a second successive Grand Slam were on their way back to Twickenham. But the Scots found their second wind. First an adventurous cross-kick from Huggan gave the fly-half Bowie the chance to score a drop-goal. 16–10. A few minutes later, Bowie gave a short pass to Will on the halfway line. He shrugged off Lowe and set off with Poulton-Palmer and full-back William Johnston in vain pursuit. Just as Lowe got back and tackled him, he touched down under the posts. Turner converted and it was 16–15 with minutes to play. As the clock ticked down, the action became more frantic. England forward Cherry Pillman suffered a broken leg as he was hacked down dribbling the ball towards the Scottish line. But the fourteen remaining England players hung on to win by a solitary point. The victory sealed England's second successive Grand Slam and their fourth championship in five years.

This was indeed a match to remember. No one at Inverleith that day could know that or anything of the fate which awaited them over the next four years. Bungy Watson would be dead within six months, drowned when his ship HMS *Hawke* was sunk by a German torpedo. Poulton-Palmer, the greatest player of his generation, was to be cut down by a sniper's bullet on the Western Front in 1915. Poulton-Palmer's winger, Arthur Dingle, was lost at Gallipoli, his body never recovered. Scrum-half Frank Oakeley went down with his submarine in December 1914. Front-rower Arthur Maynard was one of the tens of thousands who died on the Somme. And Harold Harrison and Cherry Pillman were both to lose their brothers, who were also England internationals. In all, twenty-seven England internationals died during the war.

Of the Scottish side that came within a hair's breadth of defeating the champions, John Will, the double try-scorer, was killed in March 1917 while in the Royal Flying Corps. His opposite winger and fellow try-scorer James Huggan died less than a year after the match while serving in the Royal Army Medical Corps. Fred Turner, who converted Will's last try to bring Scotland within a point of England, met his end less than ten months later in Belgium. Full-back William Wallace died shortly after transferring to the Royal Flying

Corps, while Eric Young, another debutant in the match, was killed in the summer of 1915. Scrum-half Eric Milroy was to become yet another victim of the carnage on the Somme. Twenty-five other Scottish internationals would also not return home from the war.

Yet it is doubtful whether a single one of them would have had a moment's hesitation in accepting their fate. In August 1914 they would rush to the colours with unbridled enthusiasm. They followed, and gave, orders that would lead to death without a moment's doubt. In this, they were only among the most prominent of a whole generation of young men who were willing to sacrifice themselves for the Imperial principles by which they had been raised and in whose spirit they played the game.

'London Scottish (1914)'

MICK IMLAH

In a poem from his prize-winning collection, *The Lost Leader* (2008), Mike Imlah (1956–2009) records the destiny of the London Scottish side of 1914. Imlah also wrote a poem in memory of the British Irish Lions and Scottish lock forward, Gordon Brown, who died in 2001. Another memorial poem, 'Stephen Boyd (1957–99)', contains much rugby content.

April, the last full fixture of the spring:
'Feet, Scottish, feet!' – they rucked the fear of God
Into Blackheath. Their club was everything:
And of the four sides playing that afternoon,
The stars, but also those from the black pitches,
All sixty volunteered for the touring squad,
And swapped their Richmond turf for Belgian ditches.
October: mad for a fight, they broke too soon
On the Ypres Salient, rushing the ridge between
'Witshit' and Messines.   Three-quarters died.

Of that ill-balanced and fatigued fifteen
The ass selectors favoured to survive,
Just one, Brodie the prop, resumed his post.
The others sometimes drank to 'The Forty-Five':
Neither a humorous nor an idle toast.

Happiness is a Scotland Cap

COLIN DEANS

Although Deans won fifty-two caps and captained Scotland, that was all in the future in this extract from You're a Hooker, Then: An Autobiography *(1987).*

I RETURNED TO HAWICK with a sneak impression that I had a good chance of being selected for the next game, which was against France. As soon as I was back on the Sunday I was out doing my usual road training but running through my mind all the time was the thought of whether or not I would be picked.

On the Tuesday night, when the Scottish selectors met in Edinburgh, I went down to the club to train. At the time I lived only a few doors down from Robin Charters, who was a selector, and I thought he might drop in to tell me if I was in the team. But 11 p.m. came and went without any word and I went to bed to try and sleep.

The postman didn't come round our way until about 9.30 a.m. and I had to take Val to her work and start myself long before that. But I couldn't settle. I had to ask away and raced to the house. There was the same kind of letter which had told me I was to be a replacement for Ireland but this time it contained the magic words, 'You have been selected for Scotland'.

Although I had trained and prayed for this moment for years I was still stunned. I sat on the stairs reading the words again. And of course I soon found something else to worry me, for it said I would collect a WHITE jersey with the No. 2 on it (to avoid clashing with the light blue of the French). I now wondered desperately if I could hang on to my place and pick up the traditional BLUE jersey of Scotland. Fortunately for the sake of Val's peace of mind, as well as my own, I've succeeded in doing that.

... Usually a new cap doesn't play on the Saturday before an international. After all, it would be a real blow after years of preparation to be hurt in a club game. However, I felt I needed some practical rugby after missing some games and sitting on the bench in Ireland. So I played for Hawick against Roundhay, suffered no harm, and we got a victory to boot. That night Val and I celebrated with a hoarded bottle of champagne ... and fish and chips.

The next day or two were really long. I was scared I might catch flu but I survived until the Thursday when the Hawick contingent climbed into Norman Pender's car and eventually arrived in Edinburgh, shaken by his driving but otherwise raring to go. We had a tough training session, then retired to our team headquarters at the Braids Hotel, where Scottish teams have gone for around the last twenty years. It's one of those places with its own atmosphere and the boys regard it as a home from home.

There's a certain tradition to the build-up for an international match and now that I was a member of the senior team I took an even greater interest in it than when I was merely a replacement.

After the training session we were bussed from Murrayfield to the Braids and sat down to dinner. The menu prices were way out of my range, but as the SRU were picking up the tab I soon adjusted. I still always have the same kind of evening meal before a game that I chose that night. It's prawn cocktail, scampi and fillet steak. And here's a tip for you. Always eat onions with the steak ... one of my old sprinting buddies assured me that runners always eat plenty of onions because they burn up undigested food.

We then watched videos of a couple of games, particularly one in which Roger Quittenton had been in charge. It's always handy to know on which areas of a game a ref is likely to concentrate. Then it was early to bed. I was sharing with Pender who wanted to sit up playing bridge. BRIDGE? They never taught you that at Hawick High School. Pontoon maybe, bridge never. So I was a bit of a dead loss to the big prop.

On Friday morning we were out at Murrayfield again but this time mainly for the benefit of the media who came along to get their pictures and interviews. As we were playing France, of course everyone was already writing us off as having no chance, which is the way we like it. In the afternoon most of us went down to a local club where we played pool or skittles, anything to take our minds off the task to come.

On Saturday morning I must have packed and unpacked my kit at least three times. It seemed ages until the bus came with its police escort. But once we got to the back of Murrayfield stand we could hear the skirl of the pipes and the adrenalin began to flow. There was the usual gauntlet of well-wishers to get by, wee laddies and grown men shouting good luck and, as he always is, my old P.E. teacher, Bill McLaren, standing near the team entrance.

In the dressing room I found a pile of good luck cards and telegrams – from Val, my parents, old friends – and one I particularly appreciated from Hawick Royal Albert, the town's soccer club. Eventually we got changed and I remember looking pretty dazed in the mirror with my new No. 2 jersey on. McLauchlan, leading the pack, soon cut me down to size. 'Come on,' he said, 'you'll have plenty of time to admire that after the game.'

We went out to have a look at the pitch. I remember the weather was cold and damp – not really suited to the usual French type of play, was my cheering thought. Already there were about 4,000 spectators at the ground who fired off their salutations as we tested the playing surface.

Back in the dressing rooms, while the skipper, Doug Morgan, gave a final briefing to the backs, McLauchlan took the forwards into the nearest bit of privacy, the toilets. One thing that sticks out in my mind is when McLauchlan pointed to the soles of his boots and said, 'These aren't just for getting a grip on the pitch. They're for getting Frenchmen out of the way.' It was a clear indication that he was expecting the pack to ruck any of the French who were on the ground, a technique perfected by the All Blacks and which the Scots have adopted in recent years.

At last we got into the tunnel. My mind seemed to go blank. It was 4 February 1978 but the thoughts I had were nothing to do with time and dates but purely with emotion. It's difficult to put into words, but I said to myself I'm here playing for my family, my friends, Hawick, the South and Scotland. And just then we emerged on to the pitch and there was a crescendo of sound from what seemed to be the whole of Scotland. What an experience and how worthwhile all the time spent on getting here had been.

We had a dream start to the game, and we played like men inspired. At one time we were leading 13–0, but injuries to full-back Andy Irvine and winger Dave Shedden cost us dear.

I was the only new cap in the Scots side that day and a couple of incidents stick out in my mind. At an early scrum I got the ball and then the French prop Cholley's head in my face. As Cholley was an amateur heavyweight boxing champion you can understand why I was, to put it mildly, a bit woozy for a while. Then I got a strike against the head and I was so elated that I gave a whoop of joy. The next thing I knew was that I was on the receiving end of a fair old punch on the chin.

I learned a lesson from that. A painful one, but one which I remember to this day and abide by. If you do get a strike against the head, just keep your mouth shut. Rejoice in your heart but not your speech.

With France, who were Grand Slam champions, getting back into the game in the second period we eventually went down 19–16. Our try scorers, before they were hurt, were Irvine and Shedden. That perhaps indicates how cruel fate was to us that day. Morgan kicked a drop goal, a penalty and a conversion. France got tries through Gallion and Haget, while Aguirre, their full-back, kicked three penalty goals and a conversion.

It seemed a long, long trudge back to the dressing room we'd left only eighty minutes before with such high hopes. I felt so weary I just sat down and I may have had a wee cry I was so disappointed. But at least the boys had given it their best shot and it just hadn't come off.

. . . Once we had showered and got on the bus for the official reception at the North British Hotel in Edinburgh we were feeling better – even more so when John Roxburgh, who is now the technical administrator, produced some miniature bottles of Drambuie while we were on our way. A lot of the more seasoned boys opened their bottles after the usual autograph signings for the ball boys. But I kept mine intact, not only because I had yet to acquire a taste for the stuff, but because I wanted to keep it as a souvenir in case I didn't get picked again.

We had been a bit down when we left but we all knew we had played well and we soon began to perk up. Once we got back to the North British Hotel it was a case of finding out where we were staying for the night and then McLauchlan came up to my room to tell me we were all to gather across the road at the Café Royal as soon as possible for a pint.

Well, the place was packed with French supporters, one of whom had a bugle. Somehow or other, Jim Renwick, who used to be in the Salvation Army, and was really a good musician, got mixed up with this particular supporter. The Frenchman played, then Jim took over and gave us a rendering of *Tally-ho* which had everyone in the place cheering, especially the French. We were clapped and cheered out of the place to go back across the road for the President's traditional reception. I was wearing a dinner suit for the first time – it cost me around £40 then and it turned out to be a bargain with the number of dinners I've since attended.

A Septic Finger: 'Red' Conway

CHRIS GREYVENSTEIN

From *Springbok Rugby: An Illustrated History* (1995).

RICHARD JAMES CONWAY is not remembered in South Africa as one of the great All Blacks; even the few among us who recall his name will never mention it with the awe and admiration reserved for a Kevin Skinner, a Colin Meads, a Bob Scott, a Don Clarke or a Bryan Williams. And yet, what 'Red' Conway did to ensure his place in Wilson Whineray's touring team to South Africa in 1960 illustrates the unbelievable intensity of the rugby rivalry between the Springboks and the All Blacks.

During the New Zealand trials one of Conway's fingers turned septic after an injury and his doctor told him that it would not heal in time for him to make the tour. A specialist suggested, probably in jest, that an amputation would mean quicker mending. Without hesitation Conway had the finger amputated and he played in three of the four Tests of the series.

A Great Moment: Twickenham, 1925

ROBERT COLLIS

In this extract from *The Silver Fleece* (1936), Collis recalls the outstanding day when he played for Ireland against England at Twickenham.

DURING THAT SEASON I lived the life of the famous athlete, and while it lasts it is certainly great fun. To be fit, to feel really well, to play continually before large, cheering crowds, to be recognised and pointed out in the street, to be rung up by the evening papers and asked your opinion on problems of the day, and see yourself quoted along with the Archbishop of Canterbury, Tallulah Bankhead, Jack Dempsey, Marie Stopes, or Mr Baldwin, is very gratifying to one's personal vanity. Playing for Ireland was something more to me than just getting 'a cap'. There was the pure achievement and satisfying glory after years of failure, but there was something else as well – 'Ireland' they yelled as we came on to the ground at Lansdowne Road, and for a moment we were Ireland to that vast crowd of our fellow-countrymen. I had taken my place with the 'men in green jerseys', the heroes of my childhood. It thrilled my imagination beyond the possibility of analysis.

From all the matches I played in, of all the great moments when I have lived most, the day when Ireland and England drew at Twickenham in 1925 stands out.

It was a keen February day. The sun shone, the wind had a nip in it, it was an ideal day for a big game. The Irish team lunched together at Richmond; our elderly supporters, the old internationals, ate large chunks of beef-steak, the players mostly cold beef and rice, coffee with plenty of sugar. My father, who had played for Ireland forty years before, swallowed his beef-steak and felt strong enough to take the field. We didn't talk very much, for already that feeling of weakness in the pit of the stomach that all athletes know had set in. We felt quite weak, as if the strain of running a hundred yards would tire us out; our eyes were slightly dilated, our pulses beat fast, we could feel our hearts thumping. We were all disquiet in mind and body, so we sang a few bawdy songs with good tunes. We marched out proudly to our waiting bus in the narrow Richmond street, while a large crowd gathered and gaped. Then we were off, threading our way slowly through the queue of vehicles. I looked out in a sort of dream at the Twickenham crowd in which I had so often walked to the ground myself. It seemed unreal now to be one of the actors. The people stared at us, some waved, we looked back through the glass stupidly, the bus driver hooted continually, we sang another song, 'Come all ye gay young fellows', our spirits rose. We arrived, dismounted from the bus, collected our bags and entered the enclosure behind the huge west stand, and were immediately surrounded by crowds of autograph hunters, friends, acquaintances and press people. We went in under the stand to our changing room. The air was electric with the expectancy of the thousands already above us. We started to change, while privileged supporters, selectors and messengers came in and out. Some stripped naked and lay down to be massaged, others put on their bright green jerseys, clean white shorts, and club stockings, and stood up stretching themselves, or sat quietly without a word, or got up and sat down nervously. Now each of us began to feel that glorious sensation of absolute fitness and muscular power. In each of us the lust for battle was rising. . . . Time to go out to be photographed.

As we emerged from the tunnel into the sunlight a great cheer went up from the now vast crowd that shut us in on all sides and was raised high above us. We looked up at the fifty thousand faces round about trying to pick out our friends, but all looked the same. Smoke rose in clouds from countless cigarettes.

. . . Some royal personage now shook hands with each of us, walking down the rows of players. As his hand was gripped by each nervous muscular giant and shaken heartily, a slight spasm of pain could be seen to pass across his face. Long training in the modern privileges of royalty and a fine sense of duty, however, enabled him to endure to the end, though it seemed to me he looked wistfully at his crumpled hand while W. W. Wakefield led three hearty cheers. He was then led off by the President of the English Rugby Union to a seat beside Adrian Stoop.

We went back to our underground changing room for a minute. It seemed like an age; the crowd above were stamping their feet. I felt the muscles of my arms, hard, I hugged myself. It felt good to be dressed lightly in clean new togs. I leaned against the wall, half shut my eyes, and began to wander off in imagination till I became a spectator rather than a player. Into my reverie broke a voice, calling:

'Now, *Ireland!*'

Am I really representing Ireland at Twickenham against England?

We filed out of the changing rooms; there was a stir in the crowd; then as we reached the ground a great roar met us, a second louder roar, and the English had come on after us. A moment's hush and the ball soared up and fell among us. It was kicked back into touch, the game had started.

At first it was just a great game, but as time went on both sides warmed to their work. It was like playing in a continuous roll of thunder. No spoken word could be heard on the ground. Soon we had forgotten the fifty thousand spectators, forgotten who we were and everything in the world save the battle we were engaged in. We leapt at each other, dragging our opponents to the ground, fought like bulls in the mêlées by the touch-line, ran through the air, fell tackled, scrambled up, kicked, fell on the ball, received tremendous blows, gave others. All the time our blood sang through our veins with a glorious *joie de bataille*. Suddenly Kittermaster, my rugby school friend, who felt none of these things, the queer aloof creature with a superb body who only played rugger when he was made to, slipped through and raced down the field. England scored, we were driven back behind our posts. But we weren't tired, we were mad to get at them again. We dashed out, full of resolve, but the

English centres were through us again, and before we knew where we were we were back behind our posts once more. Now we went out to battle, a long pass went to Smallwood on the English wing. I just got him with a low dive as he was starting off about the English twenty-five line. Horsey Brown was up; we kicked the Englishman off the ball. We dribbled it right under the posts. In the rush to touch it down Horsey ran into the post and was stunned. Then it was half-time. The Irish team got together: 'Forwards, you must rush them right off their feet when the whistle goes.' We set our teeth. The ball landed in the hands of the English scrum-half, but we were on him, carrying him, the ball and all, twenty yards down the field till Wakefield hurled the whole lot of us into touch with one mighty charge. But on we came, down the field, a man fell on the ball, we kicked him off, another went down, a scrum formed, we slipped the ball back, Sugden feinted twice, sold the dummy, threw a long pass to Stephenson; he raced over. Back to halfway amid a roar of triumph from every Irish throat in England. Off again; once more we did it, scoring far out – 'All square!' – a man died of excitement in the stand. The crowd had gone crazy, and the roar rose and fell like waves about us. Grimly now we fought on. I was nearly spent, I had been knocked on the head and kicked in the stomach. I was bleeding from the mouth. It was nearly time; we made one more frantic effort. Down to their line we rolled them and held them there for five minutes, but cross it we could not. Man after man was tackled within a yard, nay, within an inch of the line. We were done, the English broke through our attack, back to halfway, back to our twenty-five line, back to our goal line they pushed us. Under the posts we scrummed. In the loose Cove-Smith picked up the ball. I lunged into him but went down with a fierce hand-off, striking the post. It had checked him a second though, he was over the line but couldn't touch the ball down, for 'Jammie' Clinch had him by the throat. I rose on my knees and clutched part of him; we lifted him, fourteen stone and all, off the ground, bent him backwards, fell on top of him and held him fiercely. The whistle blew. The English got the ball out, the scrum-half threw out a long pass to Kittermaster. It didn't go quite straight, we were on him before he could move. The ball came loose. It landed in my hands, I kicked it. As I did so, a huge, vicious forward struck me, knocking the remaining wind out of my body. I went down dizzily, scrambled up drunkenly, the ball had gone into touch. The whistle blew loudly. *Time*, 6–6, a draw, honours easy, Ireland, England. The crowd broke on to the ground from all sides; we were surrounded, lifted up on shoulders, beaten on the back. Strange Irish faces appeared, and gaunt hands reached up and shook ours. People whom we had not seen for years or were never to meet again appeared for a moment and were lost. The cheering went on. At last we reached the pavilion, battered, dead beat, but completely, blissfully happy, at peace with ourselves, utterly content for a moment in time.

A Dark Blue Jersey

HOWARD MARSHALL

Howard Marshall (1900–73) describes the experience of winning a Blue
for Oxford in 1921. Subsequently he became a well-known journalist and
broadcaster. From *Rugger Stories* (1932), originally published in the *Daily
Telegraph*, 8 December 1930.

SOMEWHERE IN A drawer lies a dark blue jersey. It is torn here and there, and the white crown which it bears is frayed and a little faded. It serves no useful purpose; if I were a woman and a rational being it would long ago have been destroyed. But I am sentimental about it, with a foolish, masculine sentimentality which no woman could ever understand.

I remember that jersey when it was new, and the clammy chill of it when I pulled it over my shoulders for the first time. That moment crowned three of the best months in my life, and tomorrow, in the changing room before the Varsity rugger match at Twickenham, other men will be feeling much as I did then.

If I may judge by my own experience they will be feeling a little dazed. Everything will seem curiously unreal after so much waiting. At the beginning of the season the Varsity match is a shining and unattainable goal in the far distance. There is no chance of your playing for the Varsity until suddenly and most surprisingly you are chosen. Even then you can only play with a kind of desperate abandon, certain that you will be dropped before the next game. But gradually your place seems to become secure, and Twickenham a real possibility.

The ordinary life of lectures and tutorials and friendly gatherings in college rooms drops into the background, and everything is subordinated – tactfully, perhaps, but entirely – to one main purpose. First there is the need for keeping fit, and then there is the growing consciousness of team spirit. As game follows game confidence gathers, until only a week is left – a tedious week of inactivity just made tolerable by fantastic golf and eleventh-hour scrum practices at Eastbourne.

This waiting is most difficult of all. Before you lies an experience which you can picture with the utmost clarity. Constantly the game unfolds itself in your imagination, with every detail standing out sharply in a familiar setting. It will be a game apart, each moment of which will remain with you always. You are certain that you will treasure it as something which can never be repeated, and when you are old you will play it over again before the fire.

And then the odd thing happens. Tuesday comes and goes, leaving only the most disjointed memories. The journey in the train, lunch at a club, a stroll in the park, the songs sung in the 'bus, a broken bootlace – these trivialities you vaguely remember. And there is a moment before the game when you fidget a little nervously, trotting round the room to limber up your muscles – that you remember also – and emerging from that tunnel under the stands to run up the little concrete slope on to that amazing green turf, with the roar of the crowd in your ears.

Your opponents are on the field, too, the fellows you have dreamt about for weeks, and you seem to be in a dream still while you automatically take up your position. The referee holds up his hand – the whistle shrills. The ball rises and falls, and somehow, in your detachment, you see yourself catch it. Your dream is shattered. The game has begun.

The only memory you will have of it is a kind of diffused glory of fighting, of desperate shoving and tackling and falling, lit here and there by incidents, a familiar figure cutting through the centre to score, or a smashing wheel which takes your forwards in a furious wave to the enemy's line. And in the background a distant roar of encouragement, heard subconsciously when the battle eases for a moment. But it does not ease often; the thud of boot and body, the gasp for breath, the splendour of foot-rush and run, these blend into a dogged state of being, and 'no-side' comes upon you unawares.

It is all over so soon. The crowds are clattering from the shadowed stands, and you sit numb and without feeling in the changing room. It is finished, and nothing else matters. A fragment of life is ended.

Well, there is a hot bath, and that is good. And the drive home with friends, and the dinner in the evening, and the theatre and the dance. The numbness passes. Tomorrow you go on tour, and life begins again.

8

TIME OFF

An Arctic Atmosphere

CHRIS LAIDLAW

Chris Laidlaw won twenty caps as a scrum-half for New Zealand and went on to have a career in politics, public service and broadcasting. On the All Blacks tour to the British Isles in 1963/64, he is guest of honour at a village fête in North Wales. From *Mud in Your Eye* (1973).

꩜

A N ALL BLACK in New Zealand or a Welsh international in Wales is invariably plagued with requests to come along to this meeting or that organisation as a guest speaker. Usually the topic is chosen for you – the last rugby tour – and if it isn't then the group simply assumes that you have a sufficiently wide repertoire of risqué stories to pass the evening off. The devil of it is that the average rugby international rarely if ever gets invited to talk about anything other than rugby, and after the hundredth address it all becomes more than a little wearisome.

The classic function at which such addresses must be made is the end-of-season club dinner, which in more civilised communities occasionally admits females, largely, one suspects, as a source of chauffeurage once hubby has fallen victim to the flowing cheer of the evening. These functions are traditionally similar in Britain, Australia, South Africa and New Zealand, year in and year out.

Besides the rugby affairs the well-known player will find himself invited to openings of fêtes, flower shows and jumble sales. I could never forget being invited to open a village fête somewhere in North Wales one summer some years ago. Having arrived at the tiny village after many hours of confusing rural lanes and byways I discovered to my horror that only I, the local vicar and the teacher spoke English. It was therefore agreed that my address, such as it was (who knows what Welsh villages like hearing from a stranger?) should be translated into Welsh by the local teacher, an elderly rather baleful-looking man. After ten minutes of nothing in particular I realised that my generous platitudes were having a distinctly adverse effect upon the assembled throng. When translated, my final heartfelt thanks at being invited to attend the fête brought an ugly murmur from the crowd above the shrill voice of the translating teacher. For the remainder of the afternoon I was completely ignored by the villagers. The atmosphere was positively arctic. By 4 o'clock I decided that the best thing under the circumstances was to beat a retreat and write the afternoon off as a failure in Anglo-Welsh relations. Just as I entered my car the vicar materialised and said, 'I thought I should tell you, old chap, Mr Llewellen didn't translate your address quite accurately.' It seemed that Mr Llewellen had, in 1935, been relieved of his girlfriend in Cardiff by a very prominent touring All Black. Since then he had borne his sinister grudge, finally relieving himself of it by telling the villagers, whom he had never liked anyway, on my behalf, what a bunch of illiterate peasants they all were.

The Dalai Lama and the
Public School Spirit

ROBERT COLLIS

In 1914, the Dalai Lama sends four Tibetan lads to England to enjoy a Rugby
(and rugby) education. From *The Silver Fleece* (1936).

S HORTLY AFTER THE commencement of the term, I found myself selected to play for the Town 2nd House Fifteen. Curiously enough the match turned out to be one of the most remarkable in my whole football career, thanks to four Tibetans who formed a large part of our side.

It was only February of the year 1914. The world's values were pre-war, and men had not begun to doubt the accepted precepts of the previous age. So it was one morning in Lhasa of the Mongolians that the Dalai Lama got an idea. Whether some rumour had come across the Great Gobian Desert, or whether, while meditating on Kama and the great OM, heaven had vouchsafed to him a message, we never heard. Certain it is, however, that he decided that Tibet needed the public school spirit. So he called together the other lesser lamas, nobles, and common Tartars, and informed them that it was his will that four of the most promising boys should be sent forthwith to Rugby School. Curious as it may seem, there were no volunteers. Piqued by this apparent lack of enthusiasm for his ideas, he there and then selected four good lads and informed them that they must start at once or have their heads cut off. So, after many adventures and perils by camel, pony, train and ship, Gongkar, Möndo, Kyipup and Ringang arrived at Rugby, having acquired a certain knowledge of English and some of the necessary conventions of European life en route.

Less the full rigours of a public school life should seem too strange at first, they were placed temporarily under the protection and in the house of an assistant master, and classified in the School as 'Town.' And so one wet, cold, windy February day in 1914 the Town House 2nd Fifteen took the field, reinforced by Möndo, Kyipup, Gongkar and Ringang.

Ringang grasped the main principles of the game fairly soon and, like William Webb Ellis, took the ball and ran with it whenever the opportunity presented itself to him, though it must be admitted such moments usually occurred after the whistle had blown. Judged by public school standards the behaviour during the match of Möndo and Kyipup was abominable. They would not get into the scrum properly, and their enormous bottoms prevented the rest of us from doing so. As the game progressed they received a number of more or less violent biffs, both from before and behind, which, I am sorry to say, they took in quite the wrong spirit and became embittered, showed a tendency to bite, and other nasty traits unexpected in good Buddhists. Gongkar, being of slighter build, had been placed in the three-quarter line. Here he wandered about miserably like a lost soul, shivering. I ran up and down the field the whole afternoon tackling people – including occasionally Ringang, who was apt to run strongly in the wrong direction – till our opponents had piled up 35 points to *nil*, when, as is the Rugby School tradition, the game ended.

It's Not Cricket

FRANK C. HAWKINS AND E. SEYMOUR-BELL

*A description of 'good play' in the late nineteenth century involves
a famous cricketer well known for his own tricks.
From Fifty Years with the Clifton Rugby Football Club (1922).*

～♦

THOSE WHO PLAY the game today, or the sister code, wherein shin guards are worn, will hardly understand what enjoyment was found in rugby in the old days where one was allowed to kick an opponent as hard and as often as he could upon the legs. The ancient 'maul' was a most warlike affair, and an old Bedminster player tells of one such struggle that lasted twenty-five minutes. It was in a game between his club and Clifton, and M. M. Curtis was taking part. Midway through the 'maul' he was on the ground, and his eye was badly bleeding. 'Hurt?' asked his opponent. 'No,' replied Curtis, 'I'll go on,' and he did. Just fancy, being able to trip up an antagonist when he was going at full speed for the line – yet this was permissible. Once, when playing, a forward had to carry his brother into the pavilion suffering from an injured leg. 'Never mind,' said the former, as he left the 'pav.', 'I'll send him', speaking of the man who had caused the injury, 'after you'; and after following him all over the field he succeeded, one may fairly say, in 'kicking' him out of the game. Today it does not sound very nice, but thirty years ago it was good play. W. G. Grace played very few games of rugby; however, he did turn out once against several Cliftonians, but did not very much appreciate the results. It was the rule that whoever secured the ball from touch threw it in, naturally there was always a sharp run for possession. W. G. Grace was a sprinter of no mean speed then, and he went for the ball, led in the race by one of the Cliftonians. The latter knew his opponent was coming up behind, but he was not at all concerned, for he had laid his plans, and as W. G. Grace drew level he shot out his foot and the rising cricketer turned a complete somersault into an adjacent bank. He did not bring the ball back to the touch-line.

～♦

The Wond'rous Tale of the Haggis-heads

ALEX VEYSEY

On a tour to Scotland in 1963/64, the All Blacks encounter a rare
Highland species. From *Colin Meads: All Black* (1974).

❧

BECAUSE MEADS WAS so close to baggage-master extraordinary George
Mackenzie he takes special delight in relating the dubious deeds
committed by Mackenzie quite outside the Baggage-masters' Code of Ethics.
Clause I of that unpublished code would state that baggage-masters should
not erode the importance and dignity of the men they serve. And Mackenzie
would laugh that one off and the 'men of importance and dignity' would laugh
it off with him. As they did, wryly some of them, when, taking advantage
of the presence of the All Blacks in his own territory, Mackenzie spun the
now-famous and wond'rous tale of the Haggis-heads. One of the young All
Blacks of Whineray's team reported that as the team travelled by motor-coach
through the gathering dusk he had seen, loping over the heath, a strange fox-
like creature, red-eyed and obviously of evil intent. Mackenzie moved in, swift
as a switch of the sporran. 'A haggis!' he said. 'God, laddie, how lucky you
are to have seen a haggis.' And as the All Blacks gathered to listen he spun
the most outrageous yarn of any rugby tour anywhere. Meads was engrossed
as Mackenzie, his candid blue eyes glowing, his honesty radiating from him
with irresistible warmth, told the New Zealanders about the rare haggis of
which it was believed only a few males were left and the species, therefore,
doomed to early extinction. He asked searchingly of the All Black who had
reported the sighting details of colour, dimension, attitude. And with each
answer he nodded sagely. 'A haggis. Undoubtedly a haggis.' And then, cursing
himself for a thoughtless fool that he had not mentioned it before, he said that
the haggis head mounted was a highly-prized collectors' item in Scotland but
normally could be obtained only at great cost. But he, from a source which
for security's sake he could not divulge, could obtain a supply to satisfy the
All Blacks' requirements. He recommended walnut mounting in preference to
mahogany because the grain came up so beautifully with polishing. At thirty-
seven and sixpence, a snip. The orders rolled in. And the King Country, for
one, was to see a mounted haggis head or two at the end of the tour. In fact,

it is devoutly recorded that Stan Meads ordered two – one for home and one for the club rooms. When the reckoning day dawned and Mackenzie made his confession to a crowded team meeting at Peebles, his performance had been so professional that many a bemused All Black was uncertain still, whether the hoax was the haggis-heads or the confession. It is to their eternal credit that Mackenzie had less spectacular success when he offered to obtain cans of the first fall of snow and send them back to New Zealand at half-a-crown a can. Only one All Black lodged an order. And that was not Meads.

∾❧

Morlaès, More or Less

PETER BILLS

Jean-Pierre Rives, the iconic French flanker, arrives at the airport
for a foreign tour but as usual has forgotten something.
From *Jean-Pierre Rives: A Modern Corinthian* (1986).

∾❧

HUMOUR FORMS AN integral part of the man's character; it has always done so. Jean-Michel Aguirre, his colleague in the French international team, knew Rives at Toulouse University and played for the French Universities on a tour of Romania which both players made at the start of the 1970s. This tour was to become known as the 'Rives passport tour'.

'Jean-Pierre arrived at the airport without his passport – he always forgot something,' said Aguirre. 'There was no time to return home to collect it, but another player who had been in doubt for the tour because of injury, found he could not travel when he reached the airport. So Jean-Pierre said "No problem – I will take his spare passport."'

Pierre Villepreux, the brilliant full-back who played thirty-four times for France from 1967 to 1972, was coach to the French Universities side for that tour. He takes up the story: 'No one thought it would be possible for Rives to use this other passport. The problem was, the other player, Morlaès, who was with the Begles club, was a tall man and had very dark hair. Also, it was short. Jean-Pierre looked as different as it was possible to look – he had long, blond hair. But he said "not to worry; it is no problem." When Jean Pierre reached passport control at Bucharest airport, the man studied the passport. He looked strangely at him, but waved him through. We could not believe it.'

So for an entire tour, Rives became a player from the Begles club, named Morlaès. The ruse was maintained all the way back to passport control, prior to the departure for France, at which stage even Rives became a shade sceptical: 'To enter the country is nothing – to leave the country is more important.'

This time, the passport control staff were not so easily convinced. A swarthy, dark man, gruff voice working in tandem with an interpreter, asked Rives: 'Your hair – what happened?'

'Oh, it is nothing. I change it. This picture is old.'

A grunt. 'Uh.'

A stamp on the passport. And freedom.

Villepreux added: 'The team thought it was incredible.'

The story had an amusing sequel when the Romanians sent a side to tour in France two years later. Rives was outstanding in one match against the tourists, and afterwards was approached by the Romanian coach. In broken, hesitant French, the trainer said to Rives: 'Monsieur Rives, you are a fine player. In my country, two years ago, I see another player, so like you. He was the player from Begles, Morlaès.' And, tugging playfully at Rives' blond locks, the coach added: 'But he was called Morlaès. Funny, he was so much like you!'

❧

Playing by Numbers

PHILIP WARNER

England and Harlequins player Adrian Stoop, one of the founding
fathers of modern rugby, was never knowingly under-organised.
From *The Harlequins* (1991).

❧

ADRIAN (STOOP), ALTHOUGH long past his peak, sometimes turned out for
the Firsts in the Twenties. One of these occasions was a game against the
London Welsh. The Harlequin scrum-half was John Worton, an Army player
who eventually was capped twice for England. Before the game, Adrian Stoop
took Worton on one side and gave him a series of code numbers designed to
introduce unorthodox moves and baffle the Welsh. Worton, however, found
this list of numbers more than he could manage, and on one occasion, when
Stoop called out '432', he shook his head and called out, 'Sorry Adrian,
number's engaged.'

❧

Scrum Down on the 10.27

ROBERT COLLIS

Shortly after the end of the First World War, Collis meets the
outstanding England forward Wavell Wakefield.
From *The Silver Fleece* (1936).

❧

BY THE BEGINNING of the winter the University was once more full, and
we set about reviving the old life in earnest. My part in this was with the
'Rugger' Club. On the first Saturday, however, I was chosen to represent the
Harlequins against the United Services in what must have been the first first-
class match after the war.

The match was at Portsmouth. I remember nothing of the game, but only
of meeting W. W. Wakefield. He stood in the doorway of our compartment

the whole way from Waterloo to Portsmouth and talked 'rugger shop' without a pause.

Wakefield is the best forward I have ever played with or against, I think. His prowess on the field is nothing to that off it, however, for he holds with Adrian Stoop the record for long-distance discussion of the game. A school contemporary of Wakefield tells how the great man, while still quite young, was lolling back in a bath with his eyes half shut after a hard game and describing his exploits to the other prefects. These, apparently used to this sort of thing, slipped away quietly from the room. When they returned twenty minutes later the monologue was still in full swing.

The friend who told me the story about W. W. Wakefield's school days once travelled down with the Harlequin team to the West Country on my invitation, with the idea of getting a cheap ticket and free lunch. He did it only once, however, because Stoop involved him in an impromptu scrum practice in the corridor, putting him in the second rank and making him push against Wakefield's buttocks.

The Kiss of Death

A. A. THOMSON

Fact and fiction meet on the try-line. From *Rugger My Pleasure* (1955).

THE MOST STIRRING fictional description of a rugger match in the opposite manner that I remember comes from the opening chapters of John Buchan's *Castle Gay*, published in 1930. The game has nothing whatever to do with the story and I fancy that Buchan, who besides being one of our half-dozen best descriptive writers was also a canny Scot, simply did not want a perfectly good visit to Murrayfield to go to waste. His diminutive hero, Jackie Galt, once of the Gorbals, was playing wing three-quarter for Scotland against the visiting Kangaroos. Five minutes before the final whistle – it is always exactly five minutes – Jackie, who by this time was 'like a heroic bedraggled sparrow,' picked up a loose ball near the Scottish twenty-five and proceeded towards the enemy line, dodging, dummying, swerving until he had gone 'through the lot' and got his try in the extreme corner having left the better half of his jersey in the hands of the Australian full-back. His fate is extraordinarily like Tom Brown's.

> There he lay with his nose in the mud, utterly breathless, but obscurely happy. He was still dazed and panting when a minute later the whistle blew, and a noise like the Last Trump told him that by a single point he had won the match for his country.

Nobody can say fairer than that. There is a tale of a similar try at Murrayfield, scored by Ian Smith, who battled his way over the line with a full-back and two hulking English forwards clasping him in a threefold annihilating embrace, a kiss of death, if ever there was one. Smith lay there silent, still, utterly winded. Two laddies from the Cowgate surveyed the fallen hero.

'He's deid,' said the first in doom-laden tones.

'Ay,' agreed his companion, 'but it was wor-rth it.'

9

DOUBLE VISION

View of a Try – I

JEFF PROBYN AND BARRY NEWCOMBE

In 1991, France play England in the Grand Slam decider.
Although England win the game, France score what has been called the
greatest try ever seen at Twickenham. In Upfront: The Jeff Probyn Story *(1993),*
the England prop describes his view of it.

⤫

FOR THIS GAME there was not the overwhelming optimism of the decider a year earlier. We looked at this game rationally, knew we were going to face an aggressive, powerful and technically sound pack and backs who would shoot all over the place if we let them. We had no intention of playing a fast and risky game and knew that our control and discipline would have to see us through. It was a case of preparing for the unexpected and knowing that when France had the ball the nearest player had to be tackled. They are the best ball handlers in the Northern Hemisphere and we had to stop them gaining momentum. This was brought home to me quite vividly by a good-luck telegram from Pierre Berbizier who was going to play scrum-half for France. 'Ball, ball, ball,' he reminded me, just as he did when we were in South Africa together.

On the morning of the game I looked around the forwards at the team meeting and could see the resolution that was going to bring a win. There was a calmness which came from the assurance that we knew exactly what we were going to do and that persisted all the way into the dressing-room and out on to the pitch. I was the oldest player in what was now an experienced side and I knew this day was going to be special to me and the rest of the team.

The match will be remembered as the day England won the Grand Slam for the first time for twenty-three years and for one of the greatest French tries ever. Hodgkinson started us off with a penalty in the first minute but when he missed one not long afterwards, hitting the ball towards the south-west corner, Berbizier came into play with his 'ball, ball, ball' theme. We had actually gifted the ball to him and even though he was behind his own line he had plans. He held the ball behind his back as the England forwards drifted right for a drop-out and set off parallel with the goal-line, heading to our left. Berbizier linked with Serge Blanco, playing his eighty-fifth game and final Championship match, and the escape became fact. Lafond and Camberabero injected more pace and found more space and Sella came next. Camberabero returned, chipped over Underwood and re-gathered, and then hammered over a cross-kick. All this was being played out in front of our grasping fingers and anxious minds. We could not reach them because the whole thing had happened too fast and the ball was doing the work. 'Ball, ball, ball,' said Berbizier. And that ball came from Camberabero's boot towards Saint-André, who gathered on the bounce and scored.

We had the best of the rest of the first half and turned round 18–9 up after Andrew dropped a goal. Hodgkinson kicked two penalties, and Underwood had scored the only England try when Hodgkinson provided the extra man. That 18–9 score looked nothing like enough and the precious gap we needed was obtained with a fourth and final penalty by Hodgkinson. Still France kept coming and two more tries had them within range at 21–19 and what seemed like an hour to play. It was nothing like that, of course, but three minutes in that situation can seem like a lifetime and slowly we played out the seconds until we won.

The reaction of the players and the crowd is something I will never forget . . . it was a marvellous, magical time of celebration and just sheer relief all round that we had done it.

View of a Try – II

DEREK BEVAN WITH OWEN JENKINS

Referee Derek Bevan was a touch judge for the 1991 England–France
Grand Slam decider and gives his perspective of the famous try.
From *The Man in the Middle* (2001).

LES PEARD RICHLY deserved all his appointments and refereed one of the
finest matches in which I've had the pleasure of running touch. It was
England against France at Twickenham in 1991. Clive and I were under the
posts as England attempted a penalty. I'm more nervous behind the posts
for a kick at goal than at any other time during a game, even when I'm
refereeing. I hate it because some of the kicks are so difficult to judge. The
kick skimmed the posts and missed. I screamed across to Clive: 'NO'. Serge
Blanco, the French full back, caught the ball behind me. As touch judges we
had instructions to stay where we were until the ball went dead. Blanco had
options: he could open it out, kick to touch or minor the ball. What he didn't
want was a touch judge running in front of him. So we stayed put. He looked
up. England were waiting for him to minor the ball but off he went down the
field from behind his own line. The French were gone and I was galloping
back to my touch-line to try to keep up. I ran as fast as I could but had only
reached the ten-metre line when the French winger Philippe Saint-André
was scoring a try at the other end. Clive had stayed still the same as me so
we were both gasping for breath as we headed for the English posts. Les had
actually caught up with play but he was in a similar state near the French
kicker. It was an exhilarating try!

A Bit of Nonsense in the Line-out – I

WILLIE JOHN McBRIDE AND PETER BILLS

In the battle to be line-out king, McBride tells what it is like to be involved
in tussles with the All Blacks in a Test in Ireland in 1963.
From *Willie John: The Story of My Life* (2004).

∽

I RELAND DID NOT have a bad team, nor was it the worst pack of forwards
ever seen in the green jersey. Bill Mulcahy was captain by then, the strong
man of the pack alongside me in the second row. He was not especially tall,
but he was as strong as titanium, never bending in any respect. He was an
excellent rucking, mauling, scrimmaging type of player. I was very much the
junior partner, but we also had around us good men like Ray McLoughlin and
Ronnie Dawson who would not be cowed or frightened by the sight of the
All Black jerseys lining up opposite. Tom Kiernan, our full-back, shared such
qualities.

I was the tallest forward in the Irish pack and was inevitably seen as the
main source of line-out possession. Alas, the New Zealanders had obviously
come to the same conclusion. So the nonsense began. I went up for an early
line-out ball and was pushed out of the line. We played on and came to another
line-out and the same thing happened, so when I got to my feet, I had already
decided I wasn't going to put up with this for eighty minutes.

At the next line-out, I arranged for our line-out thrower to call for me and
prepared as though the ball was coming straight for me. It did, but I didn't
jump. Didn't move a foot off the ground, as a matter of fact, but what I did do as
the New Zealander opposite me jumped for the ball was swing my whole body
around to face him, leading the movement with my fist. It struck him deep in
the solar plexus as he was in the air, catching the ball. There was a loud sound
like 'uuuuuhhhhh', a deep groan and the player sank to the ground. He went
down so fast he made the *Titanic* look tardy by comparison. Play went on for a
while, but when there was an infringement and the referee blew the whistle, I
glanced back upfield. There I saw the player I had hit still on his knees, his head
dropped down, but with the All Blacks captain trying to drag him to his feet.

The next thing was our captain, Bill Mulcahy, said to me, 'Jaysus, McBride,
d'yer realise who yer just hit?' I said, 'I don't know but I'm not having that

150

treatment at every line-out.' Mulcahy said, 'Christ, you hit Meads – now there's going to be trouble.' Anyway, Meads was helped to his feet and he was groaning and holding his ribs area. He wasn't very well. Mulcahy's advice was, 'Just be careful for a minute or two.' Within those couple of minutes there was a ruck, and to this day I don't know who or what hit me, but I got it, smack, full in the face and I was dazed. I went down and I knew why I had got it. I could hear voices echoing around in my subconscious for a few moments, and I wasn't very well for a time. But I got up and I survived. When it came to the next line-out, no one pushed me out of the line and I won our ball.

... I believe that was the day I became a man on the rugby field. In rugby, as in life, you are faced with difficulties that require a solution. It is how you handle those problems and whether you are prepared to stand up and confront them like a man that defines your future path. I went on to that field not knowing who on earth Colin Meads was. By the end, I had a healthy respect for him and, I knew subsequently, he for me.

A Bit of Nonsense in the Line-out – II

ALEX VEYSEY

The All Blacks encounter McBride for the first time in the same game. From *Colin Meads: All Black* (1974).

IT WAS IRELAND first up and from that experience – and what was to follow against Munster and Leinster – Meads nurtured for ever a great respect for Irish rugby men. and none more than Willie John McBride who in 1974 broke Meads' record of fifty-five Tests for his country. When Meads thinks of Irish rugby he thinks instinctively of McBride for if there is one man Meads admires as much as a staunch team-mate it is a staunch opponent.

... Like Meads, McBride was an effective winner of possession without being a line-out jumper of the classical sort and it was in this area that they came to know each other well. McBride is on record as saying that Meads was the inspiration which drove him on to great things in rugby, for from Meads he learned the basic need to contest. Meads himself believes McBride – with other Irish forwards – was rugby-bred to that requirement, anyway . . . 'Our games in Ireland in 1963 and 1964 were terribly hard, especially those against the Irish international team, Munster and Leinster. They were all as Irish as a Paddy's market in the forwards, nothing defensive about them, no respect for names or reputations. Colin Meads was just another bloke to be taken on by eight Irishmen who firmly believed they could lick any man in the house. Though I didn't play in it, I ran touch in the match against Munster and I couldn't even keep out of trouble then. The crowd was right up against the touch-line and when a couple of the forwards were having a tussle there was no room for me between them and the crowd. So I tried to break them up and the Munster forward was so fired up he wanted to get into me, too. Hell, they were magnificent those little, mad men of Munster. They looked about half the size of our fellows but if it had not been for the performance of Mac Herewini, who played full-back, we'd have been beaten. Munster had a group of well-known players: the full-back was Kiernan, the fly-half was English. Murphy was on the side of the scrum, Walsh in the three-quarters. The other names did not mean much to us but by the end of the game, which we won 6–3, we knew all about Irish rugby. Though we had already played the Test, and scraped in there, too, Munster really rammed home what men can do when their hearts are in the right place. The test was my first contact with Willie McBride and he let me know early in the match and in the most basic way that he was to be no soft touch. I went down. I was a sick boy. Whineray came to me and said, "Get up Piney. For God's sake, get up. Don't let them know you're hurt. I saw it. Leave it to me. You just get up and get into the line-out." I did, but I was useless for a few minutes. Strangely enough, within that time Willie John went down, too. Whineray looked concerned – and innocent. Bill Mulcahy was McBride's locking partner and they were a good pair. I suppose if we had one distinct advantage over Ireland it was that we were a better controlled forward unit, more disciplined, if you like. But those Irish. What hard, hard men they were to play against.'

❧

Ace up Our Sleeves – I

GRAHAM MOURIE WITH RON PALENSKI

*The All Blacks are about to play Wales on the 1978 tour of Britain and Ireland
and skipper Graham Mourie does a bit of forward planning.
From* Graham Mourie: Captain *(1982).*

◆

FROM IRELAND WE went back to Wales and the change in atmosphere was
complete. Thinking of it since, it might have been because we were at
Porthcawl, 50 km from Cardiff, instead of staying in the intense atmosphere
of Cardiff itself. But whatever it was, the build-up before the Welsh Test did
not seem right.

We started well in the Test, with Stu Wilson, as we had planned, surprising
the boys from the Valleys by running the kick-off back at them but it soon
became apparent that we were being outplayed in the forwards. They were
motivated and skilful and, as occasionally happens, the incidents and drama
which make a Test match the nervous experience that it is, favoured one side.
The Welsh. A bit of a fracas involving Billy Bush gave the Welsh a penalty and
they got another when J. J. Williams – and who accused whom of acting in this
game? – stumbled into Bryan Williams. A third went their way when Roger
Quittenton made a mistake over a tackle on Ray Gravell. All we had in return
was a try from Stu Wilson, brilliantly executed. A kick to the corner by Bill
Osborne and Wilson raced Clive Rees to the ball. But it was 12–4 to them.

We drew back to 12–7 by half-time but the position was not healthy the
way the Welsh forwards were playing.

I was not too worried. I knew that the team had self-control. I was asked
later if I thought at any stage that we might lose. I replied no, because the team
had character, the confidence and the strength of mind – plus the physical
strength – to continue playing until the final whistle. Even while the Welsh
forwards were playing well, it became obvious they would not score more
points unless we gave them to them. A part of our overall policy was not
to give away kickable penalties and our discipline re-established itself in the
frenzied second half of the Test. We defended and we defended and eventually
drew to within two points. I knew we could win, but how to get the points?
How were we to score?

153

Andy Haden and, to a lesser extent, Frank Oliver have carried the burden of the blame for what came to be known as the line-out dive, for which the Welsh accused us of cheating. And which earned us a degree of criticism from New Zealanders too, taking time from their own celebrations of the win to deliver it.

I had a part of it too. Haden and I and others have always had a policy of having an ace up our sleeves, something to throw down at the last minute when the stakes are high and all else has failed to win the hand.

The previous night in Porthcawl, I said to Haden: 'Remember the time that Ian Eliason got penalties off Colin Meads by diving, at the suggestion of J. J. Stewart (then in Taranaki) from line-outs?'

Haden: 'Yes, Goss.'

I then said: 'We might need something like that sometime.'

About twenty hours later, with time ticking away, Doug Bruce once again spiralled the ball downfield, eluding J. P. R. Williams into touch. The first line-out was indecisive and Roger Quittenton ordered another. As the Welsh hooker, Bobby Windsor, prepared to throw Haden and Oliver spoke to each other.

The ball went in, Haden went out, Oliver went down. My view of it all was obscured and I couldn't ask because the noise was intense. Quittenton shot up his arm, awarding us a penalty.

Whether Oliver was held down or up by the much-maligned Geoff Wheel is something we will probably never know. The fact was he did have a hand on Oliver's shoulder. That was against the law and, as a result of Quittenton's vigilance, he paid the price. Who was responsible? Andy for acting on a suggestion I had placed in his mind the night before? Me for putting the suggestion there? Wheel for putting his hand on Oliver's shoulder? Quittenton for doing what we had selected him for? We considered Quittenton to be, if not the best referee we had encountered among the English from whom we could choose, then the most honest. Is that the fault?

Or is it the pressure of international rugby, which places such great emphasis on winning at the cost of some of the more gentle qualities of life?

It was easy later to sit back thoughtfully and say the act was not in the best traditions of the game, that we had contravened the spirit of the game. No one could dispute that – and I don't – and I know that some of the players later regretted it and their part in it. But it was equally true that in that crucial, unforgiving minute in the searing heat of Cardiff's Arms Park, the match – the Test – was won and the tour continued to its climax.

Whatever the thoughts of the rights and wrongs, Brian McKechnie kicked his way into a piece of rugby history. When you are on tour and, more especially, when you are on Cardiff's Arms Park, it is of little importance discussing moral questions. One thing alone stands in the consciousness: New Zealand 13, Wales 12. That won't alter until the end of time. The next day in Bristol as we and others discussed the game, that line-out, and read newspaper reports and heard of the debates raging on Welsh television, Lyn Jaffray came up with one question which silenced all. 'Did we win the Test?' The answer lay in one word: 'Yes.'

If we did not deserve to win because Wales had 70 per cent of the ball, they did not because we scored the only try of the Test. Where does that leave the game and the point of playing?

I learned later of an amusing sidelight to that line-out. Ian Eliason, the first diving practitioner as far as I know, was watching the Test on television at home. When he saw Haden stagger from the line-out, he shot up out of his armchair shouting, 'They've stolen my trick . . . they've stolen my trick.'

Eliason's trick was really J. J. Stewart's, and made its debut in 1966 when Taranaki played King Country in the final match of the season. Colin Meads had been bothering Eliason and other Taranaki forwards during the first half and at half-time, Stewart suggested that the ball should be thrown to Meads in line-outs – 'because he didn't jump anyway', J. J. said – and that Eliason should stagger out, yelling something suitable while doing so.

The Taranaki prop, Ian Macdonald, was finding it difficult not to laugh so Stewart banished him back to number seven, the only time in his life he played there. Meads, the injured party, was not amused and demanded of his team-mates: 'Who is pushing Eliason?' No one knew. After the game, which Taranaki won 20–12 with the help of three penalties, Meads knew what had happened and stormed up to Eliason, saying, 'That's the dirtiest trick I've ever seen on a rugby field.'

The final word belonged to Meads, however. That match was the last in a long career for referee Bob Forsyth, from Wellington, and in his after-match speech, he paid tribute to various people who had helped him during his career, '. . . and I would like to thank J. J. Stewart for all the help I've had from him.' Then came the booming voice of Meads from the floor of the hall: 'I'll bloody well bet you have.'

Ace up Our Sleeves – II

J. P. R. WILLIAMS WITH MILES HARRISON

Wales are 1978 Grand Slam winners and desperate to beat the
All Blacks at Cardiff Arms Park. But is their forward planning good enough?
From *JPR: Given the Breaks – My Life in Rugby* (2006).

᪥

IN THE AUTUMN of 1978 New Zealand came on tour to Britain and Ireland
and it prompted us to speculate that, in the year of our Grand Slam-winning
team, perhaps this would be the time for Wales to beat the All Blacks. But
who would lead the Welsh against them? My room-mate for the last ten years,
Gerald Davies, had called it a day after the Australian tour and, with Phil
Bennett and Gareth Edwards gone, it was obvious that I was in with a chance
of captaining Wales for the first time. I knew that, to some extent, I would
have been made captain by default but I would have been pretty upset had I
not been give it. I was skipper of Bridgend at the time and, when the press
informed me of my appointment, I think it did come as something of a relief.

It was not just a new captain that gave Wales a fresh look. The Cardiff
half-backs, Terry Holmes and Gareth Davies, stepped up, as they had in the
Second Test in Sydney a few months earlier. As captain I felt it was vital to
remind them of all the good work that had been done on tour and to insist
that they forget about who they were replacing and play their own game. To
their immense credit, they did just that and, 12–4 ahead at the start of the
second half, a famous win seemed within our grasp.

New Zealand had eroded that lead to only two points when, with a few
minutes to go, a line-out was called inside our half. There had been barging
at just about every line-out that afternoon but for some reason the English
referee, Roger Quittenton, suddenly saw fit to blow the whistle and award the
All Blacks a penalty. At full-back, I was not in the greatest position from which
to argue but I could tell that my forwards were mystified. Brian McKechnie
strode up and, sure enough, sent the ball through the posts to give the All
Blacks a one-point victory.

There was no live television interview for the captain in those days when,
no doubt, I would have been shown a replay of the incident, so I had to wait
until the next day to see the match footage. When I did, I could not believe

it. The All Black lock, Andy Haden, had clearly 'fallen' out of the line-out by faking a push. The more I watched it, the more farcical it looked – it was not even a good pretence. Roger Quittenton had been conned and his subsequent reasoning that he had penalised Geoff Wheel for barging into Haden's fellow lock, Frank Oliver, smacked to me of a cover up. Oliver did not even try to win the ball and, as the others fell away, poor Geoff found all of his support gone and merely put his arm across to try to balance. What made it even more disappointing was that a week after the match a patient of my father's told him that he had seen the All Blacks practising this trick at their base in Porthcawl in the run-up to the Test. If that's true, I wish I had known it at the time – we would not have contested the line-out and would simply have given them the ball!

I last saw Roger Quittenton in 2003 and, understandably I suppose, he was not keen to talk about the incident when I tried to broach the subject with him. The image of that line-out still haunts me and whenever I see it or read about it, I know there is a lot of upset there. It was the day when Wales should have beaten New Zealand. Although I admit that to a certain extent it was our own fault we lost – we were the better team and should have put New Zealand away long before Haden's infamous dive.

◦◦

It Never Rains in Durban – I

DEREK BEVAN WITH OWEN JENKINS

Derek Bevan, about to referee the 1995 World Cup semi-final between South
Africa and France, is assured 'It never rains in Durban'. But the heavens open
and the ground is flooded. If the game is cancelled, then France go through.
Much sporting and political history depends on Bevan's decision.
From *The Man in the Middle* (2001).

◦◦

DURING THE WEEK before our semi everyone was talking about the state of the pitch. Durban is a seaside town and a real surfers' paradise. When you opened the curtains of the hotel bedroom the view was fantastic, a real beautiful setting. The evening before the match the officials were invited to

157

the home of the President of the Durban Referees. He lived in a magnificent house in the mountains above the town. We had a lovely evening and we were told that the weather forecast for the following day wasn't too good, but our hosts assured us with a 'Don't worry, it never rains in Durban'. Although we only had a couple of glasses of wine I didn't sleep at all well.

The following morning, the heavens opened. A huge black cloud moved overhead and it was as if day had turned into night. All along the sea-front in Durban, traders sell their wares on the side of the pavement. When the rain came down they scattered everywhere and rushed to scoop up their belongings. There was terrific thunder and lightning. A few of us had been having a stroll and we were soaked through by the time we made it back to the hotel. It was hammering down. As the morning passed the rain didn't relent.

It was still raining when we got out to the ground and somebody suggested that I had better take a look at the pitch. The groundsman was sitting in his office with his feet up on the desk, smoking a cigarette. I asked him for a pair of wellington boots so that I could inspect the pitch. He didn't have any. He told me they weren't needed because 'It never rains in Durban'. I told him it certainly was raining if he hadn't noticed and I asked him what their plans were. They had no plans. I keep my boots in plastic bags. On that day they happened to be in Tesco bags so I put these over my shoes and strapped them to my trousers so I could inspect the pitch. It was about ninety minutes before the kick-off and my shoes were disappearing under the water. I realised that there was no way the game could proceed under these conditions. If a maul or a ruck collapsed, or there would be a pile-up, players faced a real danger of drowning. Safety is of paramount importance so I wasn't going to let anything like that happen.

I went back into the dressing room and told Clayton and Wayne that I wasn't prepared to start the game. It was still raining heavily so things were getting worse. I went back to see the groundsman who was still sitting in his office, and still had no plans. By now the IRB officials were beginning to arrive along with the teams. The captains and coaches came to see me and I told them that I wasn't prepared to start the game, and complained that nothing was being done about the situation. I had suggested a pump to clear the water, but nothing had happened.

The stadium was beginning to fill with supporters and slowly, the clock was ticking away. Terry Vaux and Brian Jones from Wales were there for the game and they popped in to say hello. I was glad to see some familiar faces from back home, as I was about to stop a World Cup semi-final from starting. Then Louis Luyt, the President of the South African Rugby Union, arrived along with Marcel Martin of France who was the Match Commissioner with the IRB [International Rugby Board]. They wanted to know what was happening and the truth was that nothing was happening. It was getting wetter and wetter and the water on the pitch was getting deeper and deeper. We were getting closer to kick-off time. At one stage we counted twenty-two people in the referees' room – and it's not a big one.

At last we had some constructive suggestions to solve the problem. The first thing mentioned was postponing the game until the following day, but that was ruled out of the question because flights were booked and hotel rooms were fixed up – there were practical reasons why postponement wasn't an option. Then someone asked what would happen if the game was abandoned permanently. Who would go through? Would it be on the toss of a coin? Everyone went diving into the rules of the competition. It was found that the result would be decided on discipline, and because South Africa had a man sent off in the game against Canada it looked as if France would then go through. Louis Luyt went white when he heard this. I was standing next to him and I could hear him speaking to the groundsman on his mobile, and he said 'I don't give a ****, get that water off the pitch now – even if you've got to drink it! Don't worry, you won't have a job by this time tomorrow if that water isn't cleared!' I then declared that the kick-off would be put back by thirty minutes.

Pumps were now sent for. The whisper had got around that France might go through if the match wasn't played. I did many television and radio interviews and was under a tremendous amount of pressure even though the game hadn't started. Everywhere I went someone was sticking a microphone or camera in my face. I went up in the lift to where all the IRB dignitaries were. There the talk was of bringing in a helicopter to get rid of the water. But then we saw the women come on to the pitch with their brushes and mops to physically sweep the water away. Everyone in the room looked very embarrassed by this.

It was obvious we wouldn't get a three-thirty kick off so we put it back again to four-fifteen. Again there were more interviews to be given but the rain had stopped. We phoned the airport for a weather forecast and they assured us that we had seen the last of the rain. That was some good news at last. The crowd was getting agitated by now because of the hour and a quarter delay, but no one left the ground. Both teams were magnificent about it and very supportive. Everyone understood the situation. If this had been a league match back in Wales it wouldn't have been played. But these were totally different circumstances: a full stadium of sixty thousand people with another semi-final the following day, every opportunity had to be given for the game to proceed. Safety of the players must come first but the pressure was immense.

The good thing was that everyone involved wanted the game to go on, so at least there was a positive attitude. The water level went down, we checked the pitch and I was happy that the game could now proceed. I had prepared myself to referee a classic but now conditions would be different, it would be a war of attrition. I told the players beforehand that there would be a lot of mistakes and the ball would be like a bar of soap. At least the conditions were the same for both sides. I said that I would try to let the game go but if a side couldn't take an advantage then I would have to blow up. This would mean a lot of scrums and I wouldn't stand for any messing about there. I would come down hard on them. In fairness to the six front row players they did very well, common sense prevailed and they didn't mess me around.

Despite the weather forecast, it rained again ten minutes into the game. South Africa scored the first try but there wasn't much between them. The game built up and towards the end France were pounding the South African line looking for the winning score. The French forwards drove on towards the try-line but Benazzi was brought down inches short and lost the ball allowing South Africa to clear their lines. Some viewed this as a controversial incident and my decision not to award a try was questioned. But there was no doubt in my mind that he hadn't scored. I've looked at it many times since then on video and I am still happy. The big plus though was Benazzi himself. When he was interviewed after the game he said he was so close to putting France into the final. I could have hugged him. He could have said something which wasn't true and the whole of France would have believed him. A camera showed he was inches short of the line. The camera had proved me wrong in the game between Australia and New Zealand in 1986, but this time it was on my side. I don't think I've been so physically and mentally drained as I was at the end of this semi-final. The French were marvellous in defeat and it was the first time that I had refereed them when they lost. I saw Louis Luyt after the game and told him 'if anyone else tells me that it never rains on Durban – I'll hit them.'

❧

It Never Rains in Durban – II

MARK KEOHANE

Chester Williams, the South African winger, waits to find out if the semi-final
will go ahead. From *Chester: A Biography of Courage* (2002).

⁓❧

FIRST WE WERE going to play, then we were told to wait, later we heard
the match could be off. If the game was to be called off, we all knew the
consequence of such a decision: South Africa would be declared the losers
because of two players who had been suspended earlier in the tournament.
Our indiscretions in a match of almost equally bizarre circumstances as the
one we were about to play in Durban would come back to haunt us. We had
had two players sent off against Canada in Port Elizabeth in a match where
the floodlights had failed and where our tempers had got the better of us.

Those anxieties could have tortured us as we waited for a decision on the
match in Durban, but Francois Pienaar, in the two hours before that World
Cup semi-final, was brilliant. He showed calmness, composure and enthusiasm.
He took the delay in his stride and made all the guys feel comfortable. He kept
focusing on the occasion and he kept channelling all the energy towards the
match. At no stage did he look rattled. He communicated what was going on
as if it were all part of the master plan.

When the match finally got underway, he kept us focused on winning. He
did not get carried away about the state of the pitch, the rain or the dreaded
possibility that it could still be called off. His entire attitude had the effect of
calming the players in what had been an unbelievably tense build-up.

I don't believe Pienaar should have captained South Africa at the World
Cup. I don't think he deserved to be there as a player. He was not the best No
6 flanker in the country and he was not the kind of captain I took to. I had
always thought he was too much flash and too little substance. My choice
would have been Western Province's Tiaan Strauss. But I will never detract
from Pienaar's contribution to our victory in the change-room that Saturday.
It was pivotal to our attitude when we eventually got on to the field. It was
crucial to us being crowned world champions a week later when we beat the
All Blacks in the final.

The chance to play in the World Cup final was so nearly snatched from us that night in Durban. We all appreciated the enormity of the decision that Welsh referee Derek Bevan had to make. To play or not to play? To risk a player's life? The field was so badly flooded that a player could easily have drowned if he had been trapped under a ruck.

While we waited in the change-room at King's Park, team officials let us know that everything was being done to improve conditions on the field, which had begun to resemble a paddy field with all the water. Even a helicopter was called in and it hovered above the ground in a desperate attempt for the downdraught of its rotors to help dry the field. Ground staff worked frantically to sweep away the water.

All we could do was wish for the rain and the water to go away. We prayed for the rain to stop, but even if it did not, we prayed that Bevan would be conservative in his decision-making and consider the huge implications of calling off a match of such importance.

Given the conditions, it would not have been an outrageous decision for any referee to cancel the game. Those conditions were the worst I have ever had to play in. The field was flooded, and in any other circumstances I don't think the game would have been played. Indeed, had it not been a World Cup semi-final I am sure the game would have been called off. But in this case it would have been a momentous decision for Bevan to have made. Even so, had he decided it was too risky to play, few would have argued against it. What would have made such a decision bold was the consequence. South Africa, the host nation, would have been knocked out of the World Cup on a technicality.

It would have been a massive decision. Bevan, though, was extremely calm throughout. We felt confident he would make the right call, which as far as we were concerned, was to play. In spite of the dangers, we felt any risk would be worthwhile that day. The uncertainty of it all, I have no doubt, helped psyche us up for that game while the French could not have cared less. If it was to be cancelled, they knew they would go through to the final and getting there on a technicality would not have bothered them.

So when Bevan gave us the okay to play France, it was as good as giving us the World Cup. I felt as if the World Cup had been taken away from us and then offered back again.

⤙❧

10

FLIERS AND DODGERS

'The Reverend Mullineux'

'BANJO' PATERSON

'Banjo' Paterson (1864–1941) was a very popular, prolific
Australian bush poet and journalist who wrote the words to
Waltzing Matilda. Revd Matthew Mullineux (1867–1945), a gritty
scrum-half, captained the 1899 British Isles tour to Australia but dropped
himself after losing the first Test. He never played for England,
possibly because of a tactless after-dinner speech in Australia.

I'd reckon his weight at eight-stun-eight,
  And his height at five-foot-two,
With a face as plain as an eight-day clock
And a walk as brisk as a bantam-cock –
  Game as a bantam, too,
Hard and wiry and full of steam,
That's the boss of the English Team,
  Reverend Mullineux!

Makes no row when the game gets rough –
  None of your 'Strike me blue!'
'You's wants smacking across the snout!'
Plays like a gentleman out-and-out –
  Same as he ought to do.
'Kindly remove from off my face!'
That's the way that he states his case –
  Reverend Mullineux.

Kick! He can kick like an army mule –
  Run like a kangaroo!
Hard to get by as a lawyer-plant,
Tackles his man like a bull-dog ant –
  Fetches him over too!
Didn't the public cheer and shout
Watchin' him chuckin' big blokes about –
  Reverend Mullineux!

Scrimmage was packed on his prostrate form,
  Somehow the ball got through –
Who was it tackled our big half-back,
Flinging him down like an empty sack,
  Right on our goal-line too?
Who but the man that we thought was dead,
Down with a score of 'em on his head,
  Reverend Mullineux.

❧

'Suddy' Sutherland

KENNETH R. BOGLE

Sutherland won thirteen caps for Scotland between
1910 and 1914 and was also a champion sprinter.
From *Walter Sutherland: Scottish Rugby Legend 1890–1918* (2005).

❧

WALTER'S HOME IN the Scottish Borders has always been a great place for nicknames. In the olden days, the Border Reivers were often better known by their nicknames rather than the real thing. Kinmont Willie, Sim the Laird, Fingerless Wull Nixon: dark men living on the edge of the law, their names used to scare children into good behaviour. The tradition endured, and endures. In the Scots Border tongue, few people used the formal 'Walter': in the streets and the factories, they preferred 'Wattie'. Likewise, the surname 'Sutherland' was too unwieldy and it was often shortened to 'Suddy' (or

'Suddie'). Everybody in the Borders knew Wattie Suddy, despite his natural modesty and unassuming nature. He was idolised in his hometown, a local hero, an icon in a tatty rugby shirt and baggy shorts. Poems were written in his honour. When James Y. Hunter wrote *A Laddie's Thoughts*, in which he imagined a young boy dreaming about his future and what he might become in life, he opened with the words:

> I should like to be a High School Dux
> With medals and books galore;
> Or swerve like a Sutherland down the wing
> To a rattling Mansfield score;
> Or watch my ball from the Cricket Field
> Right into the Coble soar.

Young boys naturally look up to great men, and so did many of Walter's friends and contemporaries. No one who saw him play forgot the experience and the pleasure it gave them. In his first season for Hawick Walter played under the captaincy of Sandy Burns, a tough little quarter-back. In an interview given many years later, Burns remembered: 'Wattie was the best player I've ever seen. He was very fast, he could swerve, in fact, he could do anything. He had great hands. He was just a real fitba' player.'

Another local man, John 'Chap' Landles, a past president of the Hawick Rugby Club, said much the same when he looked back on a lifetime of watching the game:

> [Sutherland was] one of the finest rugby players that I ever saw. There was no feature of the game that he wasn't adept at – goal-kicking, running, passing and tackling. There was no feature of the game that he wasn't top notch.

Most of the people who watched Walter Sutherland had few pretensions to high culture. They rarely went to art galleries, or to the opera, but they knew beauty when they saw it. Wattie Suddy was a player who was capable of great things, a man who aroused deep passions, who could express dreams through the accessible language of sport. There were hundreds of football players, some of them very good, but Walter Sutherland was special. Why? What made him stand out? Off the field and dressed in his civvies, he was an unremarkable person, apart from his striking fair hair, small and pale, just another young man on the high street. But once the game had started, that was a different matter. Who was ordinary or delicate then? Walter had all the essentials of a great wing three-quarter. His principal weapon was his explosive speed, his ability to scorch the ground. He was very fast and few players caught him once he had moved into top gear. In his six years of club rugby he averaged twelve tries a season, an excellent strike rate in an era of claustrophobic defence and monotonous forward play. But Walter was more than just a good finisher, a mere sprinter who ran fast with the ball. One of his friends and training partners in Hawick, Jimmy Grierson, later recalled that, 'Walter was one of the best that Scotland ever had. He could run, he was fast, but he could play rugby though.' Walter possessed a shrewd footballer's brain. He was clever, sharp and quick-thinking. He was a good kicker, both out of hand and from place kicks. One of his favourite attacking ploys was to cross-kick at speed, bringing the ball back into the middle of the field and causing panic among the defence. He had great powers of deception, which enabled him to escape from situations that looked hopeless. In attack he was an unpredictable target, possessing a subtle change of pace and carefully controlled body movements that could produce a bewildering series of side steps and swerves. He was a veritable weaver of spells who was capable of near-impossible escapes. Andrew 'Jock' Wemyss played in the same Scotland side as Walter and always kept a photograph of his old friend above his desk. One of rugby's great writers, Wemyss knew a thing or two about the game. In his time, he saw all of the great wing three-quarters, but he always maintained that Walter was one of the best, if not *the* best, comparing him with the Welsh maestro, Gerald Davies. Sixty years could not cloud his memory. In the early 1970s, he wrote:

> Besides great pace, Suddie could beat an opponent with what I can only describe as a 'stutter' on his feet. I remember Walter Forrest, Scotland's full-back, saying that the only way to stop Suddie was to tackle him before he got into his stride.

Sometimes, wing three-quarters are unpopular members of a team. They can be prima donna figures, reluctant to get their hands dirty and flinching from the hard work, but happy to grab all the glory by taking the final pass and scoring a try. Nobody ever accused Walter Sutherland of being a shirker. He was a strong defensive player and few people got past him, despite his seemingly delicate and frail physique. Tireless and dogged, he was good on the floor, always willing to mop up loose balls and courageously falling at attackers' feet. There is no sense of irony that his greatest display in the cauldron of international rugby was in a defensive role, covering the role of an injured colleague as well as his own and thwarting wave after wave of opposition attacks.

Any assessment of Walter Sutherland's reputation must take into account his personality and character. By all accounts he was a pleasant and good-natured young man who was genuinely modest about his talents and achievements. It's unlikely that he would have been remembered so fondly if he had been a boastful, superficial or empty-headed person. At this time, rugby football was strictly an amateur sport and Walter made little or no material gain from his endless hours of practice, dedication and self-sacrifice. He played the game simply because he loved and enjoyed it. His reward was the honour of representing his town and his country, and the recognition that this brought him. He played in the right spirit, always giving his best and trying hard to win but quick to praise his opponents and accept defeat with good grace. In short, he represented all that was good about rugby football. Naturally, these qualities extended far beyond the field of play. At the outbreak of war in August 1914, Walter enlisted in the army within a matter of weeks, ready to do his duty and serve his country and, if necessary, to give his life for a cause that he thought was right.

My Greatest Game: Errol Tobias

BOB HOLMES AND CHRIS TAU

In 1981 Tobias became the first black to play for the Springboks and won six caps in all. He selected the Springboks' 35–9 victory over England in the second Test at Ellis Park Stadium, Johannesburg, in 1984 as his greatest game. From *My Greatest Game: Rugby* (1994).

'HE'S NOT COLOURED: he's pure gold.' So said coach Dick Greenwood after the English tourists had scraped a 23–21 win over a Federation XV in the second match of their 1984 tour of South Africa. Tobias scored 17 of the home side's points but was hardly a surprise package, let alone a secret weapon. The Brits had been given privileged glimpses of his progress from raw teenager to mature play-maker in more than a decade of intermittent contact. He had been a Barbarian star in an epic 32-all draw with Cardiff in 1983 but among the first to spot the Boland builder's potential was Scot Andy Irvine, way back in 1974. Still wincing at the memory of the Lions' encounter with the Proteas that year, he said: 'It was an extraordinary game. The Proteas were total strangers to the laws and were kamikaze tacklers into the bargain – a lethal combination. But one member of the opposition did impress me that day. He saw very little of the ball, on the few occasions that he was given space he moved like a thoroughbred. He was young and extremely raw. But his talent shone through. His name was Errol Tobias.'

Tobias played centre or fly-half and kicked penalties. Throughout the re-public's stuttering steps towards integration, he assumed greater responsibilities – kicking goals being one of them. In the mid-1970s, he once boasted a 100 per cent record against touring sides; yet for all this, as he points out, 'traditionally they used to say that blacks cannot play fly-half – in other words, they don't have the brains . . . you know . . . to read the game. I had played fly-half for South African blacks and South African coloureds, but I still had to prove to many people that this [thinking] was wrong. I wanted to do that for my people and my country. It might seem strange and many have accused me of being a sell-out, an Uncle Tom, but in the end I had to do what I had to do. I had a point to prove, I wanted to be the one calling the moves. And this is why I have to choose the game against England, because I proved without a shadow of a doubt that I could do the job.'

. . . 'Everything went right for me that day,' recalls Tobias. 'It was a quiet build-up in the hotel on the Friday. Cecil Moss, the coach, expected the best from us, saying that a win was not enough. He asked for a classic win. "I don't want 'good'," he said. "I want a superior Springbok performance." On the Saturday, I remember the first ball I touched. It felt so good. I was feeling so light on my feet. In the first few minutes I noticed that the opposition fly-half [Horton] was nowhere near me. I accelerated and passed the ball which went to the wing. Then we had a line-out. I told Danie Gerber: "Danie, this is the day. I feel we can do it. Horton was slow on to me. Let's work on the inside-centre and try to create gaps and overlaps on the outside. Let's do it like that." He said: "OK, it's up to you, Errol." The ploy worked a treat. Danie scored soon afterwards for the first of his three tries. I got the ball from the line-out, punted and chased. The full-back [Hare] fumbled, I won the ball again and made a blind-side break to put Danie through for his first. The second Gerber try was roughly similar.'

By now, you get the idea that Tobias is playing down his own contribution, which was substantial, to Gerber's hat-trick inside seventeen minutes. Actually, it was Divan Serfontein who supplied the final pass for Gerber's second but Tobias was in the thick of it. With a rampant pack in front of him affording the perfect platform, he was now turning it on and sent the hapless England backs the wrong way for Gerber's third. 'The cover defence went for me and Danie scored unopposed,' he says. But the best moment, indeed, one of the most memorable in South African rugby history, was still to come.

'We got quick ball to Carel du Plessis from a line-out. He ran around his winger and drifted in-field where he got blocked. I remember Rob Louw arriving – what a fantastic player, you could always rely on him to be there. Our forwards joined in, started driving and Rob came out of the maul with the ball on the blind side. I shouted to him: "switch" and he came back on the outside. The ball eventually went to Jan Villet who had a real nose for a gap and he straightened and passed to me just outside the England '22'. I glanced over to the man opposite me. It was one of their centres [Palmer]. Avril Williams on the wing was also closely marked by his man [Bailey]. I realised that the try-line was near and decided to try to sell a dummy. As I moved into a semi-jink, my whole body language was saying I was going to pass to Avril but I realised he had nowhere to go. My opposite centre lowered his head too soon for the tackle so he could not see what I was doing. When I saw the back of his neck, I changed gear and went inside while handing him off. As I was doing that I remembered the words of my first coach sounding in my ears. "Don't take your eyes away from your opponent, never let him out of your sight!"'

With Bailey having opted to stay with Williams, Tobias, head tucked in, hurtled for the line. 'I could not remember at the time that I threw my hands in the air in triumph. The crowd went mad with joy. The feeling was incredible. After that we scored another try and then Heunis got injured and I took over the kicking duties as well. I landed a conversion to make it England's biggest international defeat. We knew we had played well. For a moment, apartheid disappeared. It was a magic moment when I proved my point that I was not a token black to give the Springboks a better image. It proved that I was there on merit and that was very satisfying.'

❧

The Greatest Welsh Right Wingers

EDDIE BUTLER

Eddie Butler has an embarrassment of riches from which to choose the best Welsh right wing for *The Greatest Welsh XV Ever* (2011).

⤳

THE NAMES IN the frame for this position are already in the envelope. Three of them, and now it is simply a question of sorting them into an order of preference. Not that the final selection process promises to be easy, and before the end of this chapter the confession may have to be made that Ken Jones, Gerald Davies and Ieuan Evans were thrown into the air to see which way they landed.

Being tossed around was sometimes the reality of life for our contenders, even if their position was offered as a refuge for the slight, the graceful and the nippy. As rugby clung to the tenet that it was a game for all shapes and sizes, the wing was sacredly held as somewhere beyond the reach of those of less sensitive constitution, the beasts that would casually tear apart the limbs of the beautiful. Trying a long time ago to analyse the workings of the small in a sport dominated by the large, I once asked Gerald if his elusiveness was inspired by nothing more complicated than the fear of falling into the arms of his pursuers. 'Unquestionably,' he replied. 'Blind terror took me to some very interesting places.'

The theory was shattered by the arrival of the super-wing. Jonah Lomu of New Zealand in the mid-1990s had the most revolutionary impact on the role-reversal, the hunted-turned-carnivore, but it could be said that John Kirwan had paved the way – and clattered innumerable tacklers out of his path – a decade earlier. At the World Cup of 1987 Kirwan was the sensation of the tournament, and if Lomu scattered England players in the semi-final of 1995, it was his taming by the Springboks in the final that was the story of rugby's third World Cup.

Since then, the wings of the world have been growing ever more towering, up to and beyond the two-metre mark in the case of Matt Banahan of England. Maxime Medard of France has the lupine appearance and height of somebody more at home in the pack, a suitably feral partner for Sebastien Chabal, but he plays on the wing or at full-back. Even so, the right wing position still offers a place to those lacking a trig point on their crown, although health and safety dictate that he has to be wrapped in a protective layer of muscle nowadays. If Evans was halfway to being bulked up, Jones and Davies remained, at their biggest, merely wiry.

It matters not a jot. If they had been playing now they would all have done the necessary work in the gym to survive the onslaught of players whose livelihood depends on a tackle-count. There could be no guarantee of absolute safety, but they would have an extra layer of insulation and their chances of survival would depend now as they did then on pace and balance – and fear. Muscle may be the chosen fibre of the professional game, but speed and the fear of being dismembered are still the essential fabric of rugby on the wing.

I mention this correlation between size and fear and speed because I remember seeing Ieuan putting himself through a rehabilitation programme in 1995. In October 1994 his escape mechanisms had for once failed and he was left on the field looking at an ankle pointing the wrong way at the end of his leg. Tibia and fibula had been broken, and just about every ligament stretched beyond endurance, but here he was, a few months later, just before the game was thrown into professionalism, tied to tractor tyres, dragging them behind him, flogging himself in an attempt to regain his sharpness. Was he still in discomfort? 'Hurts like hell,' he said and carried on hauling his burden through the mud.

This was not a thoroughbred at work but a mule, bending its back to recapture the gift of speed. It was not, however, punishment without reward, because in 1997 he would go on his third Lions tour, the victorious adventure to South Africa. And in 1998 he would end his club career by winning the Heineken Cup with Bath against Brive in Bordeaux. Fear drives a wing away from danger; courage pulls him back into the thick of the action.

What else are we looking for in our right wings? On his side of the field there is perhaps more of a demand to chase kicks by a right-footed scrum-half than on the left. Ploughing a furrow up the touch-line in pursuit of box-kicks, often with little prospect of laying a hand on the ball, is not what makes a fast runner volunteer to play on the wing. He dreams only of passes that put him into space, if only half a yard of freedom, in which he might strut his stuff.

He must be prepared to wait. Fewer good passes go left to right from players whose stronger guiding hand, usually the right, favours a delivery the other way. Patience, then, is a virtue, an obligation. In their day – and the three of them neatly cover every decade from 1950 to 2000 – there was a tendency to grow cold on bad days. The instruction to go looking for work had not definitively been given, and Ieuan might therefore argue that his burst into midfield for the try he scored for Llanelli against Australia in 1992, in a win to rival the Scarlets' victory two decades earlier over the New Zealand All Blacks, was ahead of its time. His celebration with his scrum-half, Rupert Moon, belly to belly, was not so groundbreaking.

No, on days when the forwards could not gain the upper hand, or when the weather was bad, or the passing poor, it was the lot of the right wing to shiver and wring his hands, and to put his head down and run yet again up the touch-line rut without the ball, with nothing to look forward to but colliding with the catcher, the full-back who has dropped nothing all day . . .

But the wing chases because it is not always a lost cause. When back-row forward Emyr Lewis, of all people, stabbed a kick through against England, the first thought through Ieuan's mind might have been that an early pass to hand would have been the better option, because Rory Underwood and Jonathan Webb seemed to have the deeper situation well covered. But off the Wales wing dutifully ran, and suddenly there was a hesitation by England's wing, a flicker of doubt, a momentary breakdown in communication between the defenders. It was all Ieuan needed, and England's lapse was converted into a Welsh try that led to their single victory in the Five Nations of 1993.

It was not quite the work of Merlin the Magician, the words used by BBC commentator Bill McLaren at the end of Evans's signature try against Scotland in 1988. If the other grand try of his career, against Australia in the final Test of the Lions tour of 1989, was a prosaic fall on the ball following an error of judgement by David Campese, whose creative bursts usually produced more positive results, this try against Scotland was a marvel. A series of sidesteps carried him from the touch-line to the goal line near the posts, a trail of blue shirts sprawled behind him. Kicks must be chased, but this try is why wings play rugby.

❧

The Two Best Backs

GRAHAM MOURIE AND RON PALENSKI

The former All Black skipper and flanker of the 1970s and 1980s identifies the two best backs he played against. From Graham Mourie: Captain *(1982).*

᠊᠊᠊᠊᠊᠊᠊᠊᠊᠊

OF THE MANY backs that I played against there were two that press strongly for inclusion in my club. Hugo Porta of the Argentine was without doubt the best. Unlike many fly-halves – to give them their more universal name – Porta was fearless, combining his courage with brilliant ball control, masterly kicking and the wonderful way he had with his running, using the ball and his body to blind the eye to his changing directions. He was outstanding with a team only just beginning to ascend the ladder of rugby nations and I wonder how good he could have been behind a top-class pack and a true international half-back. Who else could go back to defend under pressure and then use soccer skills to head a high kick into touch? That was the action of an extremely cool man, a sublime player.

My favourite French back was the wing, Serge Blanco, who sometimes had the heart of a butterfly yet under pressure was capable of unleashing an attack which could result in a try at the other end of the field. Playing for Taranaki against Cote de Basque in 1979, I cautioned the players who had little experience of French rugby of the inadvisability of relaxing for the slightest moment against the Latin opposition. With two minutes left to play, we led 13–7. Our forwards had played well, denying the French backs the opportunity to create any points by flair. A misplaced kick landed near Blanco and from inside his twenty-two, he scythed his way through our defence, dummied, burst again and scored under the posts, then coolly converted it. We thought we had a draw. But from a scrum following the kick-off, Blanco went on the short side and made a magnificent break to send a team-mate to score again, under the posts. He then converted again. From 13–7 to 13–19 in three minutes. That was brilliance, one man sweeping twenty-nine aside.

᠊᠊᠊᠊᠊᠊᠊᠊᠊᠊

An Outdistancing Brilliance: C. N. Lowe

A. A. THOMSON

Lowe played nine times for England before the First World War and sixteen times afterwards, losing only twice. His record of eighteen tries was not bettered by an England player till Rory Underwood in 1990. So, despite P. G. Wodehouse's poem *The Great Day*, which follows, someone must have passed to him. From *Rugger My Pleasure* (1955).

❧

O F THE THREE-QUARTERS, there were several men of the highest talent: there was C. N. Lowe, of Cambridge and Blackheath, probably the fastest of all English wings, and one of that select band who earned a number of caps both before and after the First World War. Though a small man, he was a heroic defender and many a giant attacker was literally staggered by his deadly tackling. He was even more famous for his prodigious bursts of speed and, perhaps, for the fact that he was far faster than any centre he played with and that he often seemed to be left out in the cold when he would undoubtedly have scored if anybody had let him have the ball. Some of his admirers said that nobody ever passed to him, just as today some of Ken Jones's admirers from Newport occasionally voice the opinion that nobody in a Welsh side ever passes to Ken Jones. Indeed, I have heard it said that Ken ought to wear, sewn to his jersey, one of those notices you see pasted to the back of new cars: RUNNING IN, PLEASE PASS. P. G. Wodehouse wrote a poignant poem called 'The Man Who Passed to Lowe'. . . . Yet I have a feeling that Lowe was no 'transient and embarrassed phantom' languishing, unacknowledged, on the touch-line; it was his own outdistancing brilliance which occasionally put him in the deprived classes.

❧

'The Great Day'

P. G. WODEHOUSE

P. G. Wodehouse was a particular fan of rugby and cricket, playing in
his school's first team in both sports and naming his most famous character,
Jeeves, after a Warwickshire cricketer. From *What Goes Around Comes Around:
A Celebration of Wodehouse Verse* (2014).

❧

I can recollect it clearly,
Every detail pretty nearly,
   Though it happened many, many years ago.
Yes, my children, I, your grand-dad,
A reserved seat in the stand had
   On the afternoon when someone passed to Lowe.

There he stood, poor little chappie,
Looking lonely and unhappy,
   While the other players frolicked with the ball.
For he knew he could not mingle
In the fun with Coates and Dingle;
   He could simply go on tackling – that was all.
I had stopped to light my briar,
For the wind was getting higher,
   When a thousand voices screamed a startled 'Oh!'
I looked up. A try or something?
Then sat gaping like a dumb thing.
   My children, somebody had passed to Lowe!

I remember how he trembled,
(For to him the thing resembled
   A miracle), then gave a little cry;
And spectators who were near him
Were too overcome to cheer him;
   There were sympathetic tears in every eye.
His astonishment was utter.

He was heard to gulp, and mutter,
   'What on earth has happened now, I'd like to know?'
And incredulous reporters
Shouted out to the three-quarters,
   'Do we dream? Or did you really pass to Lowe?'

There was sweat upon his forehead,
And his stare was simply horrid:
   He stood and goggled feebly at the ball.
It was plain he suffered badly,
For the crowd, now cheering madly,
   Saw him shudder, start to run, then limply fall.
Then a doctor, who was handy,
Fanned his face and gave him brandy;
   And at last, though his recovery was slow,
He regained his health and reason
By the middle of next season;
   But the shock came very near to killing Lowe.

A Last Look at the Forth Bridge:
Ian Smith

W. ROWE HARDING

Ian Smith won thirty-two caps for Scotland between 1924 and 1933, scoring a
remarkable twenty-four tries. From *Rugby Reminiscences and Opinions* (1929).

IAN SMITH IS probably the greatest natural wing who ever played the game.
In his best years he was good all round. He kicked quite well, and used his
pace effectively to cover not only his own wing, but the wing on the other side
of the field. He possessed not only speed, but stability. There have been other
wings as fast, but they could not, like Smith, maintain that pace for run after
run, nor has any wing in my experience combined stability with pace as Smith

did. Most fast wings are like butterflies. They crumple up easily enough if you can but touch them. Nothing but a wholehearted tackle upset Smith, and even that was often unsuccessful. To all the wings I have played with and against I will say, 'We may all be mighty fine fellows, but we can none of us run like Ian Smith.' After the Welsh match against Scotland at Edinburgh, in 1924, which Scotland won by thirty-five points to ten, largely through Smith's wonderful running, the left wing asked to be introduced to Smith, as he explained that he had not had an opportunity of seeing him during the match. Indirectly, Smith was the cause of a famous remark by the late T. D. Schofield, then one of the Welsh selectors. The day after the match the team was taken to see the Forth Bridge. 'Take a good look at it, boys,' said T. D. Schofield, 'because it is the last time any of you will see it at the expense of the Welsh Rugby Union.'

❧

The Most Beautiful Player I Ever Saw: Ronnie Poulton

A. A. THOMSON

Poulton played for England from 1909 to 1914, captaining the side in 1913/14.
From *Rugger My Pleasure* (1955).

❧

THE ENGLISH THREE-QUARTER line of 1912 must live perennially in the memories of those who saw it; apart from the swift and determined Chapman, the line might be described as the creation of the strategist and team-builder, Adrian Stoop, who was himself playing that day at stand-off half, with J. A. Pym, of Blackheath, as his partner. J. G. G. Birkett was a three-quarter with the build of a forward, a human forerunner of the Conqueror tank; to any full-back faced with the agonising problem of tackling him, he must have seemed a moving mountain.

The other wing was Henry Brougham, a dashing and dangerous fellow anywhere near the line. The left-centre, the fourth of that line was Ronald William Poulton, who was without exception the most beautiful player I ever saw. It is difficult for a lad not to have an idol, and Poulton was mine. Rugby footballers, like cricketers and indeed like most other groups of men, can fall into two broad categories. They may be puritans or cavaliers, artisans or artists, honest toilers or dazzling charmers. Both kinds are of undoubted value and the game, and the world, would be the poorer without either. But one kind is far more numerous than the other. There are many artisans (bless them all) but few artists; there are many honest toilers, but very few enchanters. And, alas, enchanters grow fewer every day.

Ronald Poulton was a cavalier, a supreme artist, a dazzler of dazzlers. There have been few like him, none quite like him. I do not know which other footballers are regarded as having consistently dazzled spectators and opponents (and, it must be confessed, occasionally friends); Obolensky, perhaps, with his never-to-be-forgotten try against New Zealand in 1936, by a breath-taking diagonal run ending on the 'wrong' side of the field; Catcheside, who leaped to fame over the French full-back's head; Ian Smith, whose speed on the wing anticipated the guided missile by half a century, and R. A. (Dickie) Lloyd who was capable of dropping a goal with virtually the second kick of a match. These were a shining company. All of them were individualists and artists with resplendent skills all their own. But none of them was like Poulton.

Cricketers are easier to assess. Everyone has an idea of what is meant by the brilliance of 'Ranji', K. L. Hutchings or Frank Woolley; the Denis Compton who flashed through the season of 1947 had it too. If Poulton reminded me of any cricketer, it was of Victor Trumper. There was in the art of both these men a swiftness, a panache, a chivalry, a sheer enchantment that caught the breath. It used to be said that the secret of Trumper's glory was his unshakeable belief that no bowler could really bowl. When you saw Poulton flying through a defensive gap that had not been there a split second before, you instantly had the feeling that the opposition did not really exist. He went through a ruck of players as the prince in some fairy tale might pass by a touch of his magic sword through a castle wall. He would move with his rhythmic stride towards a waiting full-back and, hey presto, Poulton was over the line and the unhappy back was clutching the air. The swerve was so accurate and yet so slight that you had the optical illusion of seeing him go, not past the full-back, but right through him. Spectators who stood behind the goal-line and watched him approach had a slightly different illusion; they declared that it was the defenders trying to tackle him who appeared to swerve. Poulton, as they saw him, seemed to run dead straight. Like Trumper, he had some of the swift, shining quality of a rapier. And, also like Trumper, he was a man, masculine but full of charm, whose character and personality stood right out from those of his fellows.

His school was Rugby and there was something in that. A delightful player at school, he went up to Oxford, played against Cambridge, not in his freshman's, but in his second year, and did what nobody else has done on his first appearance, before or since: scored five tries in the Varsity match. He was, in every sense of the phrase, something out of this world.

He made his début as an outside three-quarter and scored his five tries on the left wing, while Martin scored four on the right. The Cambridge defence was shattered that day. Poulton's candid friends – he had no enemies – said that he sometimes bewildered his partners by his brilliance and that his supreme individualism was just a thought too individualistic. On the other hand, the people who saw him during this period unite in maintaining that there was never a finer exhibition of combination between backs. But this problem of brilliant individualism is not always the problem some people think it is. A genius in any field of human endeavour is not likely to fit automatically into a conventional team. It may be, at the very first, that he does not fit into the combination at all; but, as the supreme ability of the genius becomes established, his partners willingly combine to give his talent a chance to flower; in other words, they give him the ball as he wants it. That is how Poulton's partners in the Harlequin or the England line saw it, and the Harlequins and England reaped a rich harvest from this understanding. After all, a brilliant individualist is not necessarily a selfish or eccentric fellow: he is more likely to be a quicker thinker and a more ingenious finder of openings than the others. He does not, as a rule, neglect his duty to the other members of his side; he merely moves more swiftly. A three-quarter line always had all to gain and nothing to lose by having a Poulton in its ranks. That old international and wise writer on the game, D. R. Gent, has said of the individualist: 'These players are laws unto themselves, and when a player like Poulton comes along, you must let him do as he likes. . . .'

I shall, of course, remember him as I saw him that day; tall, slender of limb, delicately poised as a ballet-dancer, his football boots might have been dancing shoes. His fair hair streamed in the wind, and his build was the tapering build of the ideal athlete, sturdy of shoulder, slim at the waist and below. Don-Wauchope, the great Scottish half of thirty years before, was said to practise running at great speed between posts set up in a line, like poles in a slalom race or at a ponies' gymkhana. When Poulton was on the move, he circumvented posts of this kind, but they were, of course, imaginary. An almost imperceptible change of step, a scarcely visible inclination of the body, and he was through the gap. And if there was no gap to be seen, one would suddenly appear, as if by magic.

Oddly enough, people who knew more than I could ever see from a distant touch-line, declare that he was not really a fast sprinter, like, say, Lowe or Liddell or Ian Smith or Prince Obolensky, who were all genuine flyers. Poulton deceived and deceived and deceived. Right or left, the opponents who had been jockeyed into a false position could not catch or hold him. There is an unforgettable picture of him, serenely outdistancing his bewildered opponents, swinging the ball from side to side at arm's length, 'as if he were rhapsodising on a concertina', compelling the defence to follow him spellbound. He played for England seventeen times and the internationals of the 1913–14 season were his last. The storm that swept Europe in August 1914 engulfed England. Her players of games were by no means the only men to volunteer to serve their country, but they were among the first to go. Ronald Poulton died with his regiment, the Royal Berkshires, in 1915.

A beautiful player, a character of the highest integrity, one of 'the loveliest and the best'. With his fair hair and his fleet limbs, he might have stood as a symbol of the heart of England, of Rupert Brooke's generation, of the golden young men who died faithfully and fearlessly in a war where much that was of value beyond price in an imperfect world perished, too.

A Tall Pale Wraith: Peter Jackson

JOHN REASON AND CARWYN JAMES

Peter Jackson played twenty times for England between 1956 and 1963.
He scored six tries for England and a further eighteen tries on the
British and Irish Lions tour to New Zealand and Australia of 1959.
From *The World of Rugby: A History of Rugby Union Football* (1979).

&

EVEN THEN, AT the beginning of his international career, Meads made a deep impression on his opponents. Tony O'Reilly says that David Marques, very much a product of public school, Cambridge University, the Harlequins and England, once declared crisply after a match in New Zealand: 'You know, the thing I despise most about that chap Meads is the way the terminal traces of your jock strap hang out of the corners of his mouth at the end of each game.'

But if Meads impressed the Lions forwards, there is no doubt that the Lions' backs enchanted the New Zealand public. Tony O'Reilly himself set a record by scoring seventeen tries, but he is the first to insist that there was only ever one name at the top of the entertainment bill, and that was Peter Barrie Jackson. A tall, pale wraith of a man, Peter Jackson was all subtlety and insinuation. His footwork and dummying defied belief and O'Reilly positively croons with admiration when he recalls the *legerdemain* and the *legerdepied* with which his tour room-mate baffled New Zealand and delighted his team. 'Honestly,' says O'Reilly, 'there were times when the rest of us felt like clearing off and leaving him with three billiard balls and a one-wheeled bicycle to entertain the crowd. He was incredible.

'In one match, I think it was in Auckland, he went across from one side of the field to the other, and then back again, like a shuttle on a loom,' (O'Reilly picks up Jackson's flat, slightly nasal Coventry accent, and breathes down his nose), 'before putting O'Reilly in for the easiest of tries.'

Peter Jackson had demonstrated his capacity for scoring unforgettable tries when he produced one to beat Australia in their match against England at Twickenham in 1958. It was not a particularly memorable tour, or even a very savoury one, and when England lost Phil Horrocks-Taylor, their fly-half, through injury, it looked very much as if Australia would win. However,

185

England pulled Peter Robbins out of the pack, and played him in the centre, and with Jeff Butterfield at fly-half, they simply poured the ball towards Peter Jackson on the right wing. In the end, he won the match by scoring a try that for sheer grace and artistry would have done credit to Covent Garden.

That same year, Peter Jackson had scored a try for England against France in Paris which so rubbed salt into the wounds inflicted by a decisive England victory that it was undoubtedly the catalyst that made it possible for Lucien Mias subsequently to lead his country into the promised land. Jackson intercepted near the England twenty-five and made off upfield with that deceptively easy looking stride on the right wing. Desperately, the French cover turned and gave chase and Jackson knew, far better than they did, that the leading man would catch him. Accordingly, as he approached the French twenty-five, Jackson eased ever so slightly to persuade the straining French coverer to commit himself to the tackle. Then, when he saw that the Frenchman was safely launched on his dive, Jackson simply stopped dead and waited patiently for the wretch to slither past. Then he calmly trotted infield and scored between the posts.

That gave England a 12–0 lead and the insouciance with which it was done sent the French crowd berserk at their own selectors. They turned on them screaming '*Démission! Démission!*' (Resign! Resign!) It looked as if they would storm the barricades. This caused untold anguish to a senior and extremely distinguished English newspaper correspondent, who had married in middle age and had made Paris the first stop on his honeymoon. He had installed his bride in some style in the *tribune d'honneur* and the thought of having her lynched in retribution for a smashing England victory was more than he could bear. While all this was going on, Peter Jackson was gently strolling back with the ball to afford the England place-kicker what Jackson might have modestly described as 'the easiest of kicks at goal'. England won 14–0.

Jackson scored a similar try against New Zealand in the last test of the 1959 Lions tour. He beat Bruce McPhail, Kel Tremain, Don Clarke and Terry Lineen before scoring in the corner. As Tony O'Reilly says, 'Peter Jackson was a loner. Probably the most unique winger that ever played rugby football. He scored tries which were quite breathtaking to behold. In terms of entertainment and in terms of effectiveness as a scoring player, he was the supreme example of the great joy of rugby, which is running with the ball.'

He was all of that. So much so, that the argument about how you would fit both Peter Barrie Jackson and Thomas Gerald Reames Davies into the world's eclectic rugby team will occupy the gods for all time.

His Own Man: Bert Solomon

TOM SALMON

It is 1908 and Cornwall, passionate home of rugby, have reached the final of the
County Championship for the first time. In *The First Hundred Years:
The Story of Rugby Football in Cornwall* (1983), Tom Salmon, writer and
broadcaster, tells the story of the game and some of the characters who played
for Cornwall, particularly the unpredictable centre Bert Solomon.

THE TALK IN Cornwall in the weeks leading to the game was of little else
save the prospect; and the county authorities, more than aware of the
importance of the occasion, took the unusual step of consulting the players and
asking them where they would most like the Final to be played. Redruth, they
said, and so Redruth it became, on Saturday, 28 March: the setting and the day
for one of the greatest sporting occasions that Cornwall has ever known – and,
as things transpired, the setting, as well, for Bert Solomon to inscribe his name
across Cornish rugby history in a fashion that has fallen to no one else . . .

Bert Solomon was a totally enigmatic and wayward fellow, with all the
failings and strengths that are the delight and despair of those who vainly
try to comprehend the Cornish. He was also a brilliant natural footballer. To
many of the most astute judges of the game, in his day he was incomparably
the best centre three-quarter in the land. Yet he played only once for England
– in 1910, the year Twickenham was opened, and when England beat Wales
for the first time in twelve years. After that match, or so it was said (and legend
now attaches itself to Solomon, as it invariably does to the great), Solomon
announced, 'I've finished' – as if a mountain had been climbed and there was
little point in climbing it again. There are others who say that the after-match
dinner was all too much for him, and that he felt cruelly out of place; and
others again who swear that what really put him off 'up-country' rugby was
somebody superciliously saying to him, 'How do you like your passes?', to
which he blurted out, 'Just thraw the ball out, boy, and I'll catch 'un.' Whether
or not any of these things happened is beside the point: but the fact is that
they *could* have happened. Whatever Solomon may or may not have been, he
was always, and invariably, his own man. The further fact is that he was invited
by the selectors for subsequent internationals and refused them, and he also

refused – or again, so it is said – an offer of 400 golden sovereigns to turn professional and 'go North'. Beyond peradventure, however, Bert Solomon was one of the most exciting attacking players that Cornwall has ever produced, and no one anywhere, before or since, has feinted a pass as he did. Not only were there wing-three-quarters who played outside him who actually dived for the line convinced that they had received a pass which Solomon had never sent, but there was once a referee who blew for a forward pass only to see Solomon, still with the ball, touching down under the posts.

At Redruth, however, on that March Saturday in 1908, Cornwall had more trump cards in their hand than the redoubtable Solomon. There were all the skills of Wedge and Davey, at half-back, the power of Milton and Jackson in the pack, and John Jackett, arguably the greatest of them all, already the England full-back, and who in his young days, used to go alone to the rugby ground at Falmouth and put pails around the touch-line and then, from the other half, touch-kick the ball into them, one after the other.

And Jackett's brother Dick, the fittest man ever to play for Cornwall, a great oarsman as well, thinking nothing of carrying his boat on his back all the way from Falmouth to Hayle Regatta, winning a few races and trudging home again. Nick Tregurtha was in the side, too, as he had been for all the championship matches, a man who epitomised for many all the qualities that the Cornish, across their struggling history, had come to admire – strength, dedication and loyalty among them.

... On the day of the county finals, Mrs. Tregurtha went to Redruth to see her son play for the very first time. Afterwards, she said to a neighbour, 'They nearly kilt my boy up to Redruth las' Saturday', and she never watched a game of rugby in her life again.

For the young men of Cornwall, rugby during that glowing season became a cult. If Tregurtha and Solomon could do it, why couldn't they? And they scrambled over the desolate acres which once had supported a prosperous mining industry, passed and kicked the ball around the doleful, silent engine-houses, and found in rugby football a colour and a fervour that their landscape had lost.

Rugby became, in some strange way throughout those years, a quite special inspiration – an inspiration almost religious in its intensity. It was as if it was not individuals who were finding themselves again (as people tend to do in religious revivals) but almost as if a land – or a very old nation – was rediscovering itself, and finding something at which it was especially good, during a time when so many other things had gone tragically sour.

But whatever it was, it brought 17,000 people into Redruth on the day of the final, when even 15,000 would have been less than comfortable. Young boys cycled from Penzance, there were those who walked from Penryn and Falmouth, and there were thousands more who spilled from the special trains which hissed into the platforms of the local station. The whole granite-grey town became a place of colour, a kaleidoscope of gold and black. Ribbons and flags and even flowers, which near enough approximated the Cornish colours – and before the day was done, 17,000 people had seen what they had come to see: Cornwall beat Durham by 17–3, and Solomon had done more than anybody else to make the victory possible.

'The Rugger Match'

J. C. SQUIRE

Squire (1884–1958) was a prominent poet, writer and editor. Despite his long poem on rugby, from which this is a short extract, his main sporting interest was cricket. He and his team The Invalids are reputed to have inspired the famous cricket match chapter in A. G. Macdonnell's *England, Their England* (1933)

... We are heeling the ball now cleanly, time after time
Our half picks it up and instantly jabs it away,
And the beautiful swift diagonal quarter-line
Tips it across for the wing to go like a stag
Till he's cornered and falls and the gate swings shut again,
Thirty fighting devils, ten thousand throats,
Thundering joy at each pass and tackle and punt,
Yet the consciousness grows that the time approaches the end,
The threat of conclusion grows like a spreading tree
And casts its shadow on all the anxious people,
And is fully known when they stop as a man's knocked out
And limps from the field with his arms round two comrades' necks.
The gradual time seems to have suddenly leapt ...

And all this while the unheeded winter sky
Has faded, and the air gone bluer and mistier.
The players, when they drift away to a corner
Distant from us, seem to have left our world.
We see the struggling forms, tangling and tumbling,
We hear the noise from the featureless mass around them,
But the dusk divides. Finality seems to have come.
Nothing can happen now. The attention drifts.
There's a pause; I become a separate thing again,
Almost forget the game, forget my neighbours,
And the noise fades in my ears to a dim rumour.

11

TIGHT HEADS AND
LOOSE FORWARDS

Moss Keane in Paris

WILLIE JOHN McBRIDE AND PETER BILLS

Moss Keane, the Irish lock forward, played fifty-one times for Ireland from
1974 to 1984. In this extract from *Willie John: The Story of My Life* (2004),
McBride relates how Keane celebrated winning his first cap.

THINK THE FIRST time I saw Moss Keane was when he came up to Dublin
to university, from Kerry, and started playing for Lansdowne. He was a great
man of Munster. Moss was big and he got a final Irish trial. This was in the
days when we had probable versus possibles as a trial – or rather the hopeless
against the no-hopers, as one wag put it. Anyway, I was captain of the probable
and Moss was included. Unlike the former captain of Ireland who lined up
his men in the dressing room before a final trial and sent them onto the field
with the stirring words, 'Good luck to yer all and every man for himself,' I
emphasised the need for a collective effort. Well, Moss knocked a few men
down, won line-out ball, which he was bound to do really given his size, and
overall played a good game.

Usually, the team for that forthcoming 1974 international match, which
was to be against France in Paris two weeks later, would have been published
on the following Monday, but for some reason they announced it on the
Saturday evening after the trial match. Well, Moss was chosen so, of course,
we had a celebration at his first cap. Now this was not a particularly good
idea, because if you have a celebration in Ireland, the following morning you
sometimes don't know where the ground is.

I can remember going down to the Lansdowne club around midnight and
after a night of beers we started on a few more. Now Moss Keane can drink in
this life; in fact, I've never seen anybody who can drink like him. By the small
hours, most of us couldn't even stand up never mind go to the toilet, but Moss
got up, went to the toilet and when he returned, said, 'Right lads, I'm away

home.' There was a general chorus of disapproval, with guys shouting, 'Ah no, Moss, you're on another pint here now,' but Moss said, 'No, I'm finished now. I'm going home to prepare to play for Ireland against France.' More loud cheers . . .

But Moss wasn't just heading back across the city. He was driving off towards Kildare. By car. We heard later that he was apparently doing quite well, actually managing to stay on the road although weaving around a bit, when he was spotted by a Garda patrol car somewhere out in the suburbs. They followed him for a while and then pulled him in to the side of the road. Now Moss was well known in and around Dublin and everyone loved him. The patrol officer looked in the car, saw Mossie and said, 'Ah, now Mr Keane. We've been following you a while and have reason to believe you've been taking alcohol.' Moss looked around and said, 'Officer, you know, it's been a good day.' And he explained the whole story.

He'd been playing for the probable in Ireland's final trial and had heard soon after the game that he'd been selected for his first cap. 'So you've had a little celebration?' suggested the officer. 'Just a couple of pints, perhaps?' But Mossie, who is as honest as the day is long, looked almost insulted by this suggestion and replied, 'Ah, no, officer, not just the couple. I've had nineteen pints of Guinness.' The officer looked at him, shook his head and said simply, 'Mr Keane, I wish you hadn't told me that.' So he produced the breathalyser and said, 'Mr Keane, I'm going to have to ask you to blow into this bag.' And do you know what big Mossie said? He looked at the officer and said, 'Officer, do you not feckin' believe me?' I can tell you now, all these years later, there had to be a lot of sweet-talking done to get Moss off that one. In the end, I don't think he ever blew into the bag; some sort of a deal was done. But that was Moss.

So we went off to Paris to play at the Parc des Princes on 19 January 1974. It was a disappointing outcome for us. It was 6–6 with two minutes left to play and France kicked a penalty to win 9–6. But I remember the night after much better than the match itself. Now, I don't know if Moss had ever been to Paris before, but I can tell you, he struggles a bit with English. As for French, he wouldn't know a single word of it. Not that I am a great speaker of the language, either, but I felt that, as captain of the team, I ought to keep an eye on the new caps, Vince Becker and Keane. Both incidentally, were from the Lansdowne club.

Becker, who only won two caps in his career, both during that 1974 season, went off somewhere else with friends and I was left with Moss. Now all he ever drank back home was Guinness, but you couldn't really get the black stuff at many places in Paris, so he was drinking everything else. I thought, well, he's a big man and you never know what might happen, so I'll keep an eye out for him. Well, we must have covered most of Paris that evening and Moss had a big night. Sometime after midnight he said he'd got a big hunger, which seemed strange because we'd been to the official banquet at the Grand Hotel and they don't exactly stint you there on portions. But Moss wanted to eat and I thought that was good, because I'd prefer him to be hungry rather than thirsty.

We found a street with a lot of little cafés and shops – I think it was in Montmartre – and I parked Moss up against this wall, because by now he was weaving around a bit, what with all the funny drink he'd had and wasn't used to. I said I'd go and get some chips or something and he was to wait there, outside the shop. Well, my French wasn't good and it seemed to take a long time to make the guy understand I wanted a really big bag of chips. Anyway, Moss kept putting his head around the corner, staggering into the shop and asking what was happening. In the end, he couldn't contain himself any longer. He came into the place and saw that the guy was also selling frankfurters. Moss waited until the guy turned his back and then grabbed one of the frankfurters and headed out of the shop.

The trouble was, Moss didn't realise that the guy was still cooking the frankfurters and forty-five of the wretched things were still attached to the one Moss had grabbed and was eating. A trail of frankfurters ran across the floor of the café, like a moving army of ants. I'm standing there with my mouth open (not because I'm hungry, just through astonishment) and the guy then turns around and sees this stream of his frankfurters disappearing around the corner out of his shop. He went berserk, absolutely berserk, as only the French can. Arms waving, shouting, appealing to whichever god he worshipped: the whole thing. There was a terrible commotion. Soon, we heard the dreaded sound of the police sirens. The gendarmes were on their way.

Moss and I stood with our backs to the wall – incredibly, he was still trying to eat as much as he could – and there were people and frankfurters all over the place. I said to Moss, 'Keep your back to the wall, Mossie. We can fight what's in front of us, but we can't fight anyone behind us.' But I don't think it came to warfare. The gendarmes, recognising two big Irish rugby players still dressed in dinner jackets and black ties, realised who we were and what had happened. It was smoothed over somehow and we went back to our hotel, never to hear any more about it.

A Pretty Heavy Dinner

JEFF PROBYN AND BARRY NEWCOMBE

In *Upfront: The Jeff Probyn Story* (1993), the former England prop describes the
post-match festivities of the 1988 Calcutta Cup game in Edinburgh.

❧

IT WAS A pretty heavy dinner afterwards. I think there was a bottle of Scotch
every three or four places at the dining table, plus wine, and most people
appeared to be throwing it back like there was no tomorrow. We had all played
a hard game and were in the mood to have a good night together, Scots and
English. I know that Dooley went to bed early, that Damian Cronin had his
face in the soup, and that a food fight had taken place. The speeches were over
when someone had the idea that we should go out on the town in Edinburgh
and when we set off the Calcutta Cup came with us. The Calcutta Cup is
part of rugby folklore because it is fought for annually between England and
Scotland, and this precious piece of silverware disappeared into the night and
could be seen being passed around the players in the street as if in a seven-
a-side tournament. The Cup was taken to a pub called Browns where it was
passed around again but on the way back it was used for dropped-goal practice
in the street and suffered accordingly. By the time the security men recovered
it the damage had been done – and Richards and Scotland's John Jeffrey were
subsequently disciplined for their part in the affair.

❧

A Shopping Spree: Rives' First Cap

PETER BILLS

In 1975, the French flanker Jean-Pierre Rives wins his first cap against
England and has a Friday afternoon to while away in London.
From *Jean-Pierre Rives: A Modern Corinthian* (1986).

꙳

AND SO THE call came, after initial uncertainty on the part of the selectorial
team. Rives says: 'Whenever I saw any selectors, they would say to me,
"How tall are you?" Always, I put three centimetres more on my height. I said
"I am big". And always I added five kilograms to my weight. They said "It
doesn't seem so" – but I was not too worried. Jean Salut had told me it was the
same with him. His reply had always been, "I am like Jean Prat" (the Lourdes
back row player who won fifty-one caps for France, as player and captain, from
1945 to 1955). So, after a little time, I said the same.'

The selectors should have known what sort of an unpredictable, rare
example of the species they were going to get from Rives' build-up to his first
international for his country. Most players confess to nerves, paying unusually
close attention to the small details which become superfluous with time. For
the new cap, in normal cases, there is the obvious concern for the game, the
desire to follow established trends, the early bed the night before the big game.
For Jean-Pierre Rives, virtually none of those aspects applied.

Rives was to win his first cap, against England at Twickenham, on 1 February
1975. It was his debut at the ground which Skrela calls 'the temple of rugby',
and before an audience of 70,000. Daunting for some, but not for Rives.

He says: 'We trained on Friday morning, outside London, and then had
lunch at our hotel. In the afternoon, I think it was usual for players to sit
around, talk, play cards, or rest in their rooms. I expected to do that.

'But when we finished lunch, Claude Spanghero, our No. 8 who had already
won seventeen caps, said, "Come with me, Jean-Pierre". So we went together
to a meeting of the players, and the officials said, "Who wants to go shopping?"

'For me, I didn't care about shopping – I thought I would rest in the hotel.
But Claude whispered to me "Say yes, say yes." So I put up my hand and said
"I want to go shopping." Claude said "I want to go, too." I think we were the
only two.

'We went to London by taxi and went to Soho to a striptease all afternoon. We paid £1 and then after the curtain went down, another £1. We stayed all afternoon seeing big, fat girls. After some hours, we realised we had to go for dinner with the team – but we were late. When we returned, the officials said, "Why have you been so long shopping?" And then they saw we had no parcels. "You have been so long but you have bought nothing."

'So I said to them, "Oh, everything is so expensive in England. I looked a lot but I could not afford to buy."'

The team officials were equally unsuccessful in getting the pair off to bed early that night. Rives goes on: 'After dinner, Claude Spanghero again said to me, "Now we go off – come with me".

'We sat up until three or four o'clock in the morning, playing poker. The other players went to bed at 10.30 – we were up for hours after.' Once again Rives had shown his predilection for the contrary; the unconventional, non-conforming role. The trait was to remain constant throughout his career.

❧

Cutting a Swathe

JOHN REASON AND CARWYN JAMES

A variety of antics at club level are revealed in this extract from The World of Rugby: A History of Rugby Union Football *(1979).*

❧

FAR, FAR BENEATH these luminaries, but enjoying the game just as much, was the infinitely various world of junior rugby, though some of the physical specimens playing it were so ancient that they would have been distinctly flattered to be associated with anything junior.

. . . This world had no frontiers and the escapades of its inhabitants have passed into folklore of the game. The Old Millhillians once misbehaved themselves on an Easter tour of the West Country, led by Bill Gibbs. From time immemorial, touring rugby clubs have encountered these little difficulties with local hotels, and on this occasion, the management firmly asked the Old Millhillians to leave. This they did, but because of the Easter holiday, found it impossible to find alternative accommodation. Accordingly, W. D. Gibbs, who became the forty-eighth president of the Rugby Football Union, and who was then Mayor of Bromley, telephoned the hotel he had just left and enquired if, by chance, they had any accommodation available. He explained that he was the Mayor of Bromley, and he had a civic delegation with him.

The hotel manager was delighted. 'Well, it just so happens . . .' he said. So His Worship the Mayor, complete with Rolls-Royce, sailed back to the hotel and booked the entire party back in again. It was some time before the hotel management discovered what had happened, but they smiled and put up with it.

The staff of the imposing North British Hotel in Edinburgh did the same after Peter Robbins had led Coventry on a Scottish tour which still brings wrinkles of anguish to the extensive forehead of that club's distinguished president.

Coventry had played in Glasgow and had celebrated their victory by cutting a swathe right across Scotland to Edinburgh. The fact of Coventry winning was not surprising, because they were then one of the most powerful club sides in the world, but they were not noted for their spirit of adventure when it came to touring. Robbins had other ideas, and was relaxing in the state room of the North British at half past seven in the morning, enjoying a bottle of best claret and reflecting on a memorable night, when he was joined by one of Coventry's more earthy forwards.

A waiter materialised out of the background, and asked the newcomer if he would like some refreshment. 'I'll drink what the skipper's drinking,' he said.

Back came the waiter with the claret, which he offered for inspection before lovingly easing the cork out of the bottle. He then poured a little of the wine to be tasted.

At this, the earthy gentleman in question leapt out of his chair, and jerked the terrified waiter two feet off the ground by his collar and tie, and snarled, 'You pour me as much as the skip's got, or I'll smash yer face in.'

Danie Craven also maintains that part of his slight baldness is due to the hair he lost worrying about some of the brighter escapades of a joint Oxford and Cambridge team on tour in South Africa a few years after. These culminated in something of a disaster when a bed was being lowered from the seventh floor of a hotel in Durban, with the idea of manipulating it back in to another bedroom on the sixth floor. For some reason, it has always fascinated touring rugby teams to empty completely the room of one of their fellows.

The bed-lowering operation is always a tricky manoeuvre, partly because the furniture removers are invariably giggling uncontrollably at the time, and this one went down with all hands. The bed escaped their grasp and crashed to the ground below, narrowly missing a fearfully expensive Mercedes motor-car, and mercifully failing to kill any of the passers-by. However, the hotel manager was not amused.

The next morning, the manager of the team rushed to present his apologies. He led a solemn deputation which assured the hotel manager that the damage would be paid for, that the culprit had been discovered and that he would be sent home at once in disgrace. The chances were that the culprit would be sent down from his University and his career ruined! The hotel manager subsided from righteous indignation to sympathetic horror in about five minutes, and the South African Rugby Board picked up the bill.

❧

A Night Out in Lyons

W. W. WAKEFIELD AND H. P. MARSHALL

The Cambridge University authorities are not keen that the 1923 side should make a tour of France. This extract from *Rugger* (1930) allows you to judge if they were justified.

❧

WE WON OUR first match against Lyons, though before we started the game we had to pick stones and glass off the field. There we were splendidly entertained, for apart from interesting visits to various factories and the local aerodrome, we were invited to dinner by the students of the Université de Lyons. They gave us sweet champagne and curious cakes, and they made fulsome speeches and sang songs. Fortunately, Hamilton-Wickes was a passably expert French linguist, so that he replied with great success. After a time the speech-making began to pall on us, and we left the hall, followed by about two hundred of our hosts, singing loudly the songs which had become favourites of ours on the tour.

We led the way towards the town, proceeding by means of short sprints and climbs up lamp-posts, and somehow we reached the bridge which crosses the river. This river, as you probably know, divides Lyons into two, and we wanted to get back to the centre of the city; however, we found that the bridge was held by a squad of gendarmes, who would not let us pass, and told us so with many gesticulations and much twirling of luxuriant moustaches. We asked why, and were told that no man is allowed to sing in the streets of Lyons. Accordingly we decided upon a policy of passive resistance, and sat down, the whole two hundred of us, in the middle of the road, smoking and playing cards. This caused the gendarmes considerable uneasiness, as the traffic was held up and the populace were becoming impatient. Reinforcements were rushed up by car and bicycle from the local gendarmerie, but they could produce no law which forbade resting in the roadway.

Eventually they decided that arbitration was the only means of ending this somewhat absurd situation, and they told us that if we would leave the middle of the road we could sing to our hearts' content. As we were tired of sitting still and also of singing, we agreed to pass on our way, but for variety we instituted a mock funeral, and marched in single file and silently towards our objective. The inhabitants were thoroughly mystified by this strange bare-headed procession in dinner jackets, and as we passed through the streets we implored all the passers-by to remove their hats, which they did with every mark of respect.

When we arrived outside a café in the centre of Lyons we decided that we no longer felt funereal, and our leader, knowing the ground, dashed through the café and out into a street on the other side. We followed, but the gendarmes, with their bicycles and cars, were not able to do so, and we made good our escape. We then thought that a little dancing would not come amiss, and accordingly visited the best dancing club in the city, only to find that our friends the gendarmes had forestalled us, and were lined up outside to forbid our entrance. The English members of the party, being possibly more accustomed to dealing with police, crept quietly away and hired taxis, in which they drove up to the club as if they were private patrons, and were at once admitted. The Frenchmen, seeing the success of our ruse, followed our example, but by that time the gendarmes had realised what was happening, and were once more forming an impenetrable cordon round the door. That evening was an unqualified success.

From Lyons the team had a wonderful run in a charabanc, but I followed with some friends in a small and very light French car. I have never been so terrified in my life, for the road was rough, it poured with rain, the surface was greasy and we skidded and swayed round corners at an enormous pace. Somehow we managed to reach Oyonnaux, where we found the town had taken a complete holiday in our honour. Flags hung from every window and all business was at a standstill, so that I was particularly sorry that the day turned out to be miserably wet. We had an extremely cold and unpleasant game, and at half-time, while we were shivering and bemoaning our fate, our opponents brought three or four fresh players on to the field, who, being warm and dry, had no difficulty in piercing our somewhat sodden defence, though we had already piled up enough points to win.

When we got back to the hotel we found that baths were an unheard-of luxury, so that we were forced to wash the thick mud off in small basins of tepid water, with disastrous results to our tempers and the hotel carpets.

At Grenoble we were also greeted by a most enthusiastic crowd, and though we were told that we should be beaten by the Sélection des Alpes, we managed to get home fairly easily. It was on the next visit that when the forwards decided to use their feet particularly relentlessly the leader cried, '*Doucement, doucement!*' or 'Gently, gently!' which corresponded by arrangement with 'Feet, feet!' with the result that he was extremely popular, but the rest of the pack were regarded as brutal and ignorant savages.

At Lyons on the return journey David MacMyn and one or two others left the train to get some refreshments, and they went over in their shirt sleeves to a bar some three platforms away. While they were inside they saw the train moving out of the station. As they had left behind in the carriage their coats containing all their money and tickets, they were naturally alarmed, and I shall never forget the magnificent spectacle presented by MacMyn as he rushed wildly over lines, points and platforms, shouting powerfully, 'My God, what shall I do? What shall I do?' and eventually getting entangled with a line of signal wires and falling flat on his face, while the train quietly backed into another platform.

Before the next season started I had a novel experience in the way of training. C. H. Prowse, a former Cambridge golf captain, was at that time doing pig-breeding on a large scale, and he invited me for a weekend to his farm. He had thirty or forty young half-grown pigs, who had to be caught and ringed. I was detailed to help in rounding them up, and I soon found that they were extremely difficult to get hold of, as they were very fast, and ran with a curious jinking movement. The only way to make sure of them was by a real rugger tackle, taking care not to break their legs and also to see that they did not cut you with their sharp hoofs. I had become quite an adept by the end of the afternoon, and for anybody not quick off the mark in flying tackles I certainly recommend pig-catching.

❧

A Magnificent Occasion

DEREK BEVAN WITH OWEN JENKINS

Post-match rugby celebrations at their best, according to referee
Derek Bevan in *The Man in the Middle* (2001).

❧

SCOTLAND AGAINST WESTERN Samoa was a magnificent occasion. I had two Australians running touch, Sandy (Macneil) and Kerry (Fitzgerald). As I'd only had pool matches in 1987, this was to be my first in the knockout stages. Murrayfield was full and Princess Anne was there to cheer on Scotland. The Hastings brothers and John Rutherford were part of a very talented Scottish side captained by the hooker Colin 'Very, Very' Deans. His nickname came from his habit in after-match speeches of complimenting the opposition by saying it had been a 'very, very hard game and you made it very, very difficult for us and we were very, very surprised to win'. It was an amazing game. Samoa kicked off, Scotland caught the ball and Gavin Hastings ran smack into the Samoan forwards. This was to be their game plan, to take on Samoa up front. It was very demanding to referee. There were huge hits going in and it was physical, confrontational but good, honest, hard rugby with flair as well. It was a pleasure to be out in the middle with the teams. There was no nonsense, decisions were accepted and it was a game where a referee could impress. When I played advantage each side took it. Scotland won but Western Samoa made them fight all the way. They lost 28–6 but at the end of the game, they made a lap of honour and received a standing ovation from the crowd. I knew from the assessor afterwards that I received a good report and that night I was going to enjoy myself. The reception was to be at Watsonians, home club of the Hastings brothers. The Samoans hadn't had a drink of alcohol all through the tournament: they had concentrated fully on their rugby. They had really wanted to do well and although they were disappointed they felt they had made their mark: they had progressed further in the tournament than had been anticipated. I'd refereed my first quarter-final and I hoped I'd made my mark, too. Theoretically these were two of the best eight teams in the world.

What a night it was! The camaraderie was magnificent, so were the speeches and the fun involved. The banter between the two sides was hilarious. We had watched France play England on television after the game and the Scots knew their opponents in the semi-final would be the English in Murrayfield, so they really let themselves go, knowing they had a week before that momentous game. Out of all the after-match functions I have attended, this stands out by far. The speeches were comical and the Western Samoans wore the kilts. There were gifts from each side to the other – everything was in the true spirit of the game. The manager of the Western Samoan team was drinking what he called 'orgasms' and in his speech he said that he hadn't had so many 'orgasms' in all his life. They had enjoyed themselves so much that they requested to stay on for a few more days, but their pleas weren't heard by the tournament organisers.

Women, Liquor and Parties

CHRIS LAIDLAW

Hospitality towards touring teams is welcome but can be a crafty ploy, according to the former All Black scrum-half in *Mud in Your Eye* (1973).

FROM THE VERY first moments of the thunderous, tumultuous welcome given the team on their arrival, the New Zealand rugby players became public property. Even the private life of Christiaan Barnard was thrust to page three as the All Blacks were pictured, pestered, pondered, prodded and praised until every man, woman and child in South Africa knew that this player ate eggs for breakfast, that one ate spinach, this lock-forward visited the toilet twice a day and that one twenty times. The world at large was fed intimate truths on the progress in Graham Thorne's marriage derby, the reasons for Earle Kirton's daily visit to church, Gerald Kember's taste in clothes, and many a member's taste in women. Skeletons tumbled from cupboards, the contents of which until then had remained confidential even in New Zealand. Invitations, nay demands, poured in for players to visit this school, open that fete, address this meeting, or simply be seen at that function.

New Zealanders, even publicity-hardened All Blacks, are rarely equipped emotionally to cope with life under a twenty-four-hour spotlight, and for many it was an unreal and very unsettling experience. Good as he might have been in some respects, manager Ron Burk simply didn't realise the importance of protecting the players from the stress and exhaustion of too many social engagements, most of which were worthless diplomatic charades designed to boost either the ego or the profit of the organisers. Towards the end of the tour social tempers became progressively frayed. Even Jazz Muller, one of the world's most obliging human beings, remarked: 'If you send me to one more school you can send me on to the airport – I'll be off!'

Women, liquor and parties – the three hardcore elements of a rugby players' fun – were but a telephone call away and sometimes closer. The Transvaal Rugby Union, with a suitable combination of warm hospitality and dastardly cunning, provided a suite in the All Blacks' hotel complete with girls, music and a cache of booze that gave one the impression that the All Black tour must have been running concurrently with a convention of hoteliers. It was here and in similar paradisial scenes that a number of All Black wills cracked, and the team for the first time in at least ten years appeared to divide into two camps – the triers by day and the triers by night. Terry McLean made a great deal of this in explaining the All Blacks' failure when the chips were down, and McLean, no sluggard when it comes to finding social reasons for physical failures, was right. In defence of his victims, however, it should be said that the very social environment of South Africa is enough to drive a Baptist preacher to the bottle.

Without the telly, and with every good movie thoroughly shredded by a paranoiac film censor, what can any visitor do but resort to the bar if he has no wish to be badgered by autograph hunters, photo-seekers and a variety of assorted nuisances who lurk outside every hotel door? For the first few weeks the New Zealanders weathered this storm with patience and dignity but as the weeks wore on other outlets simply had to be found and the inevitable occurred.

12

LAST LINE OF DEFENCE

A Rugby Genius: W. J. 'Billy' Bancroft

J. B. G. THOMAS

In *Great Rugger Players 1900–1954* (1955), J. B. G. Thomas gives a
graphic account of Bancroft's rugby personality and explains
why his reputation was so high.

RUGBY FOOTBALL HAS had several outstanding personalities, and many of them are Welshmen, but perhaps the most legendary of all is William John Bancroft, of Swansea. One of the oldest international players, he still retains a vital interest in the game and can claim to have watched every representative match played at the famous St Helen's ground. In Swansea he is something more than a legend – he is an institution. Ever since rugby was first played on the St Helen's ground, Bancroft has been there, as ball-boy, player, critic, watcher, and now as one of the ground officials. It is a remarkable record of service to the game, and it runs like a thin red vein of life-blood through Welsh football. Bancroft has either watched or played with everyone of fame associated with the game!

Still as outspoken now as he was in his playing days, and just as confident in his judgement, he was the first of the great full-backs, and down through the years has never had to watch a superior! There have been many great ones, like Gamlin, Strand-Jones, Marsburg, Morkel, Johnston, Nepia, Crawford, Drysdale, Bassett, Owen-Smith, Jenkins, Norton and Scott; but none of them really possessed all the outstanding qualities of Bancroft, which enabled him to make thirty-three consecutive appearances for his country over a period when there were no visits from touring sides. This is by far the longest record of appearances by a representative full-back, and he achieved this between the ages of twenty and thirty-one.

Bancroft was not a giant in frame, like Marsburg, or Gamlin, or Jenkins; but a dapper little man, immaculately dressed and groomed. He well deserved the title of 'Beau Bancroft' at the time, for his spotless attire, well-brushed hair and trim moustache made him appear something of a dandy on the field of play. Indeed, his appearance was such as to encourage opposing forwards to 'have a go' at him, only for them to find his amazing speed, sense of position and cradle-like hands enabled him to outwit them time and time again. Bancroft was a rugby genius, and like Gould, the other star of the Welsh back division during the era, he feared no man on the field, and preserved a confidence that was cool and determined.

He was in many ways incredible, for he performed feats on the field which, although they can be regarded now as rugby legends, were nonetheless daring at the time of execution. He could not be judged by ordinary standards, for he could do so much more than a normal international player. He could field a ball on the run with remarkable accuracy, and then, while still running, send it to touch wherever required; cross-kick accurately for the benefit of his side; or even drop at goal.

Perhaps the greatest memory he left when he retired was that of disorganising and reducing the power of opposing packs of forwards. A ball would be kicked ahead to him just inside his own half, where he would gather it, but instead of the traditional widening of the angle before kicking to touch, he would nonchalantly dwell a pause for the attackers to get on to him. Then, just as it appeared he would be tackled and downed with the ball, he would slip away tantalisingly across field with the speed of a darting snipe, leaving his pursuers clutching at the air. In a moment they would turn and chase again, only to see Bancroft repeat his 'disappearing act' with all the elusiveness of a magician!

After several similar manoeuvres, he would suddenly essay a kick to touch, and leave his opponents exasperated, and often with bellows to mend. It was a remarkable performance, which used to bring the house down whenever Wales played at home, and almost reduced the opposition to tears. He specialised when playing against Irish forwards, and enjoyed 'taking the Mickey' out of two grand Irishmen, the Ryan brothers. For years he worried them, but one day they caught up with him! It was at Cardiff Arms Park, and they threw him, ball and all, into touch! Of course one cannot say that Bancroft would get away with such tactics against modern back-row forwards; but I think he was clever enough to have evolved some method of worrying even the most persistent of modern No. 8s.

A great number of stories are told about Bancroft and his 'brushes' with opposing forwards. Dai Gent tells a very good one about a well-known Devon county forward who went to Swansea with another county player as members of the visiting side. Like many other forwards, they had played against Bancroft several times, and had run many miles, but never to catch the wily little Welshman. This time they meant to capture him and teach him a lesson, but half-time came and neither forward had laid a hand on the wary 'old fox'. They were so disappointed that they decided to 'down him' whether he had the ball or not!

The chance came near the end of the match, for Bancroft had held the ball until they were about to tackle him before putting in his relieving kick. The fact that he had kicked did not arrest the charging Devonians. They crashed him to ground in violent manner. 'Let go!' shouted 'Banky' to his attackers. 'The ball's gone!' Back came the heated reply, 'And so are you!' as they flung him through the air. There was an appeal by the Swansea players, but the referee, sensing the situation, ruled that it was a simultaneous tackle and no penalty kick was awarded. Even though their side had lost the match the two Devon forwards were seen to leave the field as if they had scored a great victory! At least they were two lucky fellows who had laid their hands upon the elusive Bancroft!

❧

Learning to Punt and Tackle

GEORGE NEPIA AND TERRY McLEAN

Nepia has an enduring reputation as one of the All Blacks' greatest full-backs. In this extract from *I, George Nepia* (2002) he tells how he learned his trade.

❧

IT HAS BEEN said that one of my special contributions to the 1924 tour was my tackling. Would you believe it, there was one particular reason for this. Elder Moser watched me one day a year or so before the tour. After the game, he tapped me on the shoulder. 'When you tackle, open your eyes,' he said. If he had not said that, I would not have won that praise in 1924. I do not think I would have been with the team. 'Open your eyes'... it sounds funny, but that is the most important of all the bits that go into the good tackle.

... All of the time, unimpaired in enthusiasm, I worked at both the spiral kick and the tackling. As a former gridiron player, Elder Moser never ceased to astonish us with his skill in throwing the ball. He held it close to one end and threw it over his shoulder, not with the long unbroken sweep of arm we had been taught but with a chucking motion, exactly as if he were throwing a cricket ball. As the ball left his hand, he would flick his fingers down and off it would sail, for fifty or sixty yards, spinning like a top. Not many of us could kick the ball as far as he could throw it.

Having watched this, I started to think of the possibility of imitating this spiralling motion with a punted instead of with a thrown ball. Paewai, Tipi Kopua, our centre three-quarter, and I used to remain after team practice kicking to each other and on one of these days I suddenly fired off a perfect spiral kick. (We used, incidentally, to call it 'The Bullet'.) I had by now made up my mind that such a kick was not feasible and when it came off I was shocked and so excited that I had difficulty in sleeping that night. I could scarcely wait to get to the field next day and I was, I can tell you, tensely excited when I had my first kick. Awful! I had another. Still awful. I slowed down my swing and gave the ball an easy thump. It wobbled horribly, a dreadful kick. Never had I known such disappointment. Not having told anyone what I was aiming at, I was too proud to ask for help or sympathy. I wasn't too proud to keep on trying, all the same, and night after night I thought about the way the foot should swing into the ball, the way the hands should hold and drop it and the height at which I should attempt to kick the ball for the sake of length, power and accuracy. This was a double-sided operation. Naturally, I wanted to master 'The Bullet' with both the left and the right feet and this meant adjusting, or transposing, each set of theories I was working on. Most interesting, most exasperating – but it had to be done. What Elder Moser could do with his hand, I was going to do with my foot – somehow. So on and on I practised. I found it a help, at times, to train at the manoeuvre of catching the ball while running back toward my own goal-line and of stopping, turning and getting my defensive kick away a split second before taking the tackle of the following-up forwards. My team-mates were always willing to help at this, even to the extent of getting a very fast man to follow up the kick. Without boasting, I would say that I got pretty good at this. It took timing and confidence and training was a great help to both. I found, too, that sometimes the spiral kick could be made accurately from a defensive position like this. It seemed that if you did not try too hard on a particular manoeuvre, it was easier to perform. But I was not satisfied with haphazard success. I wanted to have that kick at call, under any circumstances.

It came, eventually. As part of my stock-in-trade, it meant a great deal to my standing. But it did not come overnight. I worked and worked and, gradually, it was mine. And I would say now that the spiral, 'The Bullet', is the cream on the coffee of good punting. A player aspiring to the first class must have it.

In the realm of kicking, the influence of Elder Moser was that I envied his hand-throw and set out to emulate it. He may never know that he was the inspiration. In the realm of tackling, however, he was the direct instructor. From him I learned all, to him I owed all.

It happened that, in my first two years at M.A.C. [Maori Agricultural College], I had to do a good deal of tackling, the more so when I eventually was posted to the midfield backs. I have told how I lost my fear in football while playing at Nuhaka a year or two before. I therefore did not shirk the task of tackling. The difficulty was that I was always knocking myself about. Being game, I would go headlong into my man; being uninstructed, I would come out of the crash with a clout over the ear or a belt on the eye or a thump on the jaw. Always something – and usually it was a good crack. Our normal practices, do you see, were the matches with senior backs and third-grade forwards against senior forwards and third-grade backs and these were conducted as if some of our ancestors had been meeting some of our other ancestors, with neither set of ancestors having much liking for the other. This was a he-man's game – and very often, so it seemed to me, I saw all the stars in creation after making head-on tackles of some of the characters on the other side. One of the senior forwards was especially tough. He came at me like one of those chariots out of Ben Hur.

Elder Moser could bear it no longer. He held me back after one practice in which I had, according to custom, seen most of the heavens, though it was still broad daylight. 'George,' he said, 'you are doing everything wrong. You should not go down and wait for him. With his speed and weight, he will always knock you over. He might knock you out, too. The thing is, when he is a couple of yards from you, crash into his stomach with your shoulder. You won't then fall back, as you usually do. You will knock him backwards. The air will go out of his lungs and you might even knock him out, too.'

We practised the Elder's theory. It was a good one. He was not, of course, elderly, though to our young eyes he did look a bit long in the tooth (I suppose he might have been in his late twenties). The point was that he was young enough and fit enough to put these ideas into active practice and it was on him that I did this early tackling.

It seemed to me I had got the whole idea right. 'Now,' I said, 'what happens if the other chap comes at me a second time?'

'Don't go for his stomach,' Elder Moser replied. 'If you do, he will probably elbow you on your head. Go below his knees. Move into him from about the same distance as before, then hit him hard. You will knock his legs from under him and he will come down hard.'

We practised, and it was so.

I said: 'What about a third time? What do I do then?'

'There will be no third time,' said Elder Moser. 'If you have made both your first and your second tackles the right way, the third time he will kick.'

Two days later, we had our usual practice game and I was, I confess, nervous about how these methods of tackling would succeed. Just before half-time, the big forward who used to make a set at me got the ball and, breaking through, headed for me. He weighed fourteen stone, he was hard and he had a mean temper. I did not have time to think. I flew into him. My shoulder hit him fairly in the pit of the stomach. He flew backwards, I on top of him. He was knocked about a bit, though he wasn't concussed. He said: 'You look out, the next time.' I knew what he meant.

At half-time, Elder Moser came to me: 'A perfect tackle, ehoa,' he said. 'Now don't forget the second time. You will be all right. Don't worry.' Don't worry! If he only knew.

The game started up again. The big forward got the ball, well away from me, but he circled until he had me sighted. Then he came at me. He had murder in his eyes.

From a couple of yards away, I crashed into him below his knees, took his legs from under him and put him down with such a heavy thud on the broad of his back that he was knocked out. He came to, a sick man. The game went on. A third time, this chap got the ball. He happened to be right in front of me. I waited. I was ready. But I was not called. As Elder Moser had prophesied, the man kicked.

It happened a little time after in an important club game that I made one of these head-on tackles unsuccessfully. I was shaken up, quite hurt, in fact. After the game, Elder Moser came up to me. 'You deserved that,' he said. 'You closed your eyes.'

'What?' I said.

'You closed your eyes. Just before impact. The result was, you didn't know when you were going to hit him.'

By Jove, I thought, he is right. I could recall that tackle vividly – my waiting for the man, charging into him, throwing myself forward and then, bang. By closing my eyes, I had ruined the timing of my tackle. It was as simple as that. Simple – and yet of tremendous importance.

I could not attempt to estimate now how many were the tackles of this sort which I made during my career. What I can say with perfect confidence is this: if you tackle the right way, they always kick – the third time.

❧

Most of All Nepia

DENZIL BATCHELOR

A character sketch of Nepia in 1924 when he played in every game on the
All Blacks tour of the United Kingdom.

❧

LOOKING BACK THROUGH the arches of the years, it isn't the niceties of technique that stand out in the sunshine that followed that morning rain. It was the heroes – George Nepia and Marcus Frederick Nicholls, the Brownlie Brothers; L. J. Corbett and H. J. Kittermaster, Wakefield and Voyce and Cove-Smith.

Most of all Nepia. The New Zealand full-back was nineteen years old, and he was the only man in the side who played in every match of the tour. He was only five feet nine inches high, but he was that phenomenon among athletes, a massively built man trained as sharp-set as a greyhound. He seemed to be made of mahogany. His legs were new-stripped glistening tree-trunks. His head, set on his short neck which would have buckled a guillotine, was crowned with blue-black hair, brushed back over his scalp. He had the poise of a panther: always on his toes, bent forward to spring to the kill. His eyes were no adjunct to a smile. They were forever staring unwinkingly to the horizon, in the search for prey: the eyes of a falcon. He tackled with the sound of a thunderclap, and punted low and deep, gaining fifty yards with a wet, heavy ball with contemptuous ease in the teeth of a forward foot-rush. His unique feat was to gather a ball off the toes of a phalanx of forwards and – disdaining to fall on the ball – smash his way with it, generally backwards, through the whole ravening pack. He had played five-eighths for Hawkes Bay, learning to open up the game for his three-quarters. New Zealand only bothered to choose one full-back for their touring side. If they had chosen one half as good as Nepia he would have done the job for them.

~

The Greatest Welsh Full-back

EDDIE BUTLER

There have been many great Welsh full-backs, and Butler makes his selection for The Greatest Welsh XV Ever (2011).

~

BUT HERE WE come back to the three initials that stand apart: JPR. The surname – Williams for the record – is an optional extra. For defiance, there has never been a player so uncompromisingly dismissive of his own welfare. Here was a doctor with a total disregard for personal safety. The tackle that clattered Jean-Francois Gourdon into touch in the corner in the Grand Slam decider of 1976 would by today's requirements to use the arms be quite illegal. On that day it was heroic. The speed with which he flew from full-back into the mayhem of the fighting on the 1974 Lions tour would by today's disciplinary procedures be reprehensible. At the time, his appetite for the fray warned the South Africans that they could win on no front.

It is tempting to say in the quest for an all-round view, that if he could catch and tackle with a technical precision to complement his lust for contact, he could not float like Blanco. He could not cut a line like John Gallagher or Christian Cullen of New Zealand, or beat a tackler with the laconic ease of the new sensation, Kurtley Beale of Australia. But JPR counter-attacked with a spirit bordering on the maniacal, and if he did not make tacklers regularly appear foolish he often enough left them in a heap. The rock under the high ball could be transformed in a flash into a mad pirate.

He was not a brilliant kicker. On the other hand, when it mattered most he put boot to ball from forty-five metres and dropped the goal that squared the match that secured the Lions that one and only series win in New Zealand. The final Test in 1971 in Auckland: New Zealand 14, Lions 14. Everybody on both sides rubbed their eyes. JPR raised his arms and wheeled away as if it had been the most natural thing in the world. He couldn't in everyday conditions kick the ball half the distance of Lee Byrne, but it was as if he knew that he had one launch – and just the one – in his system and that he had better choose the moment of release with care. He had an instinct not just for the recklessly valiant but also a nose for the unexpected.

He wasn't perfect. In 1981, having retired from the international game at the end of the golden age of the 1970s, he attempted a comeback. In truth, he was not the player he once had been. Looking mortal did not become him. History, though, can be kind, shrinking that unfortunate period into a fleeting error of judgement, to be buried beneath the memories of what he was at his peak.

∽&

The Pinnacle

GAVIN HASTINGS WITH CLEM THOMAS

Captain of the British and Irish Lions on the 1993 tour of New Zealand,
Hastings pulls a hamstring, which makes him doubtful for the crucial
second Test. From *High Balls and Happy Hours* (1994).

∽&

AFTER AN EASY win against Taranaki, we then went on to play Auckland in what everybody regarded as the fourth Test. I got carted off with a hamstring injury before half-time, and we went down 23–18, with the remarkable Fox again kicking most of his goals. We found ourselves in the disheartening situation of suffering three consecutive Saturday defeats. To make matters worse, we went on to Hawke's Bay, where the midweek side got badly beaten on the Tuesday before the second Test, and that was undoubtedly the lowest point of the tour. A number of the guys were injured, myself included, and I was not sure if I would be fit enough to play in the second Test. The team against Hawke's Bay had performed really badly and morale at this stage was very, very low.

Raising the spirits of my team was all the more difficult because I was injured, but I told them that it was all a question of knuckling down. The team for the second Test was not announced until the Thursday afternoon, because I was not sure of my fitness and there was the question of playing Scott Gibbs in place of Will Carling. There was a doubt concerning my ability to get on to the field and I believe Geoff Cooke wanted to keep a position open for Will Carling, because of his captaincy experience, in case I did not make it.

Finally, the team was announced, with me being named although I was getting physiotherapy treatment around the clock. I went out on the Friday and I remember that all the tour supporters, about 600 of them, had come out to see us. It was a nice morning, a bit damp under foot, and we jogged three lengths around the posts; I thought, 'There is no way I can play tomorrow', because I could feel my hamstring niggling away. So I went up to Ian McGeechan, with all the photographers and their huge lenses focused on me, and said, 'Geech, look, I won't be able to play in this game tomorrow.' Firmly he said, 'You are playing tomorrow.' So we called in Geoff Cooke and Dick Best, and I repeated my doubts, but again Geech said, 'Look, I don't care if you come off after two minutes, you are going on to the field.' So I said, 'Okay, to blazes with it, I'll lead the team out.' I then gave a press conference, with the reporters asking why I was not practising goal kicking. I said, 'You will notice the ground is very wet under foot and very muddy. Athletic Park will be completely different and it will be firm, so there's no point in my kicking today.' Basically, I bluffed and flannelled my way through the press conference, and everyone accepted that I was going to play, although they may not actually have believed it.

During the game I could still feel my hamstring, so I decided to play myself in gently. When we were awarded a few free kicks, I got Rob Andrew to take them to touch and eventually I had a couple of penalty kicks at goal. I missed the first two, which was not really surprising as I had not been able to practise for the whole week. After that, I put a couple over, just before half-time, and all of a sudden, having been on the field for over half an hour, I had gained in confidence and knew I was going to stay on for the whole game.

I had won the toss and Geech and I had decided previously that, because of an incredibly bright sun, we would take the dangerous decision of playing into the wind and the sun. We both felt that it would probably be the best way to get the team to focus themselves and it worked, for the Lions concentrated and played some great rugby into the elements. Our forwards easily won the line-out battle and one of our most important tactical decisions was that, instead of kicking for touch, we would keep the ball in play. This, together with the fact that we put the All Black scrum under pressure, was crucial.

The only problem in the first half came when Grant Fox put up a Garryowen and, standing on my goal-line, I lost the ball in the sun. Eroni Clarke got the bounce, which beat Scott Gibbs, Rory Underwood and Dean Richards, all of whom had got back in support, and he scored for Fox to convert – the Lions were trailing 7–0 after thrity minutes. The All Blacks never scored again and it said a great deal for our discipline that we never gave away a single penalty for Fox to turn into points. He had not failed to kick a single penalty in any Test match for five years, so that was some achievement. Having missed my first two penalties, one of which hit the post, I made no mistake with my next two, and just before half-time Martin Bayfield won the line-out, and Morris's fast pass gave Rob Andrew the opportunity of dropping a superb left-footed goal.

Early in the second half I kicked a third penalty, before we scored a corking try from a blistering counter-attack. Dewi Morris began it by seizing on a dropped pass inside his own half. He made the break and, straightening up, gave it to Jeremy Guscott who, with his incredible ability to inject pace, beat Frank Bunce and forced John Kirwan to check. He now flicked on to Rory Underwood, who tore up the touch-line, past John Timu, for a superlative and spectacular try in the corner. If only his dive for the line had been as good as his fifty-metre sprint! I kicked another penalty goal and we had actually given the All Blacks as big a hiding as they probably have ever had at home, or anywhere else for that matter. Nobody ever scores millions of points against the All Blacks, but that 20–7 victory was the most points that the Lions ever scored in a Test match against them.

I came off the field on a huge high and went up to Geech and gave him a big kiss. I said, 'Thanks to you I was part of a great experience and, if I'd called off the day before, I would have regretted it for the rest of my life.' He said, 'I knew you'd make it and that you would be all right.' It is a funny thing but in the heat of a moment and with the adrenalin flowing, you can get through. I suppose the damage was less to the hamstring than it was to my mind.

13

NO-SIDE

Why Do Men Love This Game?

A. A. THOMSON

In the last chapter of *Rugger My Pleasure* (1955),
A. A. Thomson summarises his feelings for rugby.

WHY DO MEN love this game? A rugby footballer is the last person in the world to answer such a sententious question respectfully. I do not know the right answer, but I am fairly certain that the sort of answer that the psychologists give would be wrong. So many theories of modern 'knowledge' are rather like BBC kitchen recipes which usually fall into two categories: if they resemble those of your grandmother, they are superfluous and, if they do not, they are uneatable.

Similarly, many modern theories of human conduct suggest something entirely foreign to human nature (at its best or worst) or something which, if true, is a long-winded setting-down in sesquipedalian pseudo-scientific terms, of something which earlier generations had known for years but called by simpler names. Psychologists may say that people play a game in the first place because it is a recreational activity of their social group. That should go down well in Wales, where so many footballers are miners, policemen, schoolmasters, tinplate workers, clergymen, engine firemen, journalists, milkmen and medical practitioners. A nice social group, to which I should be honoured to belong. They may say that people play rugby football because it is an atavistic symbol of a desire to return to the cave-man habits of their ancestors; because it is a sublimation of their destructive instincts; or because (I have heard this theory seriously advanced in a high-pitched voice) they are steeped in sadism from their bourgeois cradles. And there are our old friends – dear old pals, jolly old pals – economic frustration and sex repression, which are responsible for so much that is brightest and best in contemporary life. Now all these reasons may be described polysyllabically as so much psychological gobbledigook; they may also be described monosyllabically.

It may be argued more reasonably, if not more scientifically, that normal intelligence does not usually lie in spending eighty minutes of a cold, darkening winter's afternoon chasing an object as irresponsible as Gilbert's 'elliptical billiard ball', whose every bounce is the acme of irrationality; floundering in mud, splashing through puddles, and being unceremoniously manhandled at the undoubted risk of broken bones, twisted knee-joints, and a jaundiced view of life. Why, it may be reasonably asked, do they do it? There is only one answer and an irrational one at that: they do it because they like doing it.

Here is a game of grace and skill, reaching, at its best, high aesthetic standards. It is also a game of such vigour that, for the sake of the Queen's peace, for very life's sake, it has to be a game of sportsmanship and good temper. If it was not, it would not survive as a game for a season. It is sometimes rough; it is occasionally naughty, though, to be fair, the authorities have pretty strict rules for dealing with naughtiness. But consider this: here you have a tremendous fellow, a Birkett, a Wooller, a Ted Woodward, strong, weighty and completely determined that nobody should stop him, going hell-for-leather for the line. Consider, too, an equally tremendous fellow, a Gamlin, a Nepia, a Bob Scott, standing at back to guard his line; he is the last warden of the citadel and his duty is both clear and desperate. Here the two of them are then: the irresistible force and the immovable obstacle. When they meet, something must happen. There is an almighty collision: a collision of willpower and manhood. There is no compromise, no reference to arbitration, no formula for a makeshift solution. They cannot even call on the kindly offices of Sir Walter Monckton. Either the winger must burst through to score or the back must bring him down. It is death or glory, or, as we say in Yorkshire, muck or nettles. The impact is terrific and if it could not be solved in all good temper and good sportsmanship, self-control and self-discipline, it would be solved by homicide, by the Puritan critic's 'bloodie murtherings'. The game of rugby football is as knightly as jousting in the lists at Camelot, at which the contestants also sometimes got hurt.

❧

The Most Innocent Means

ROBERT LYND

In *On Brutality* from a collection of essays *The Goldfish* (1927), Robert Lynd argues that 'rough' games such as rugby have valuable qualities of innocence.

❧

NO ONE CAN deny that rugby football is rough. No one can deny that men constantly get hurt when playing it. I have seen games that had to be stopped three or four times while a player obviously suffering excruciating pain was rubbed and tugged back into something like normal life. A rugby football field is a battlefield on which nobody is supposed to hurt anybody, but on which people inevitably get hurt. If you judged the game by its worst accidents, you would sign petitions to the Government to suppress it. What must Sir Hall Caine have thought when he read the description of the last international match between Ireland and Scotland – a match that was played in the mud during an icy blizzard, and, what with the rigour of the game and the rigour of the weather, resulted in two players being carried unconscious off the field and, if I remember right, in the swooning of the referee? Compared to such a game, an ordinary prize-fight would seem like a Sunday-school entertainment. And the truth is, rugby football cannot be defended except on the assumption that it is good for young men within limits to treat one another violently and to take part in contests of strength and skill that tax human endurance to the utmost.

There may be moral heights from which all contests for supremacy seem odious, but we do not live on them. We match team against team, man against man, horse against horse, and dog against dog, and we rejoice in the beauty of the strength and skill that triumph in the contest. It would, perhaps, be better for the race if we could devote ourselves entirely to intellectual and spiritual pursuits, but that for most of us is not the alternative to strenuous pastimes. If boys and young men give up rugby football, it will scarcely be in order to study *Hours with the Mystics* or to lead the lives of hermits. Games are the alternative, not to a better kind of employment, but to a worse kind of idleness. They are among the most innocent means of enjoying life and of making it dramatic.

The Best of All Possible Worlds?

ALEC WAUGH

What is it about rugby that causes young men to spend many dark winter
Saturdays getting to and from obscure places where they can expect only
extreme discomfort? An extract from *The Young Man's Game* from
On Doing What One Likes (1926).

❧

A T THE BARRIERS of innumerable platforms, at innumerable stations, you
will see between the hours of a quarter past one and two on every Saturday
afternoon throughout the winter, small groups of people with brown bags
clustering round a man who stands with a notebook in one hand and a packet
of railway tickets in the other, clustering in response to a card sent out on
the previous Tuesday. 'You are selected to play for "B" SV, v. —. 1.23 Victoria,
meet barrier 1.10. Tickets taken.' They have done, the majority of them, a stiff
morning's work. They have had no time for lunch. They have rushed, on their
way, into a pub for a ham sandwich and a glass of beer. The train is packed; for
one half of the journey they will probably have to stand; they will find on their
arrival that no one knows the map reference of the ground, and scouts will be
sent in search of a friendly native. The game, they at last find, is to be played
on a bleak windswept field with a converted army hut at the far end of it. Three
other sides are already in possession of the hut. They find such corners for their
clothes as may be still untenanted.

It is dark by the time they return there seventy-five minutes later, bruised
and muddy and exhausted, with the game lost or won. They wash, a limb
at a time over a small tin bowl of lukewarm water. One lamp is suspended
precariously from the ceiling and in its uncertain light they search despairingly
for socks and collar studs and ties. But at length everything is found, and the
side move in mass to the station, arguing out the game, explaining how a
fifteen-point defeat was actually a moral victory. They commandeer a couple
of third-class smokers and search in the stop-press column of their evening
papers for news of what the 'first' has done.

They linger awhile in Victoria at the bar, while the team begins gradually
to disperse to its homes, its parties, the routine of its private lives. They know
very little of what each does with himself during the remainder of the week;

that is the curious thing about the rugger world; it is a world of its own hardly more than recognising the existence of the other world. You may play with a man right through a season without knowing his profession or his address, his income or his upbringing; which is no bad thing for it ensures the acceptance of each man at his face value.

Gradually the team disperses. In a little while only some half-dozen are remaining at the bar, and they think that it is time they were moving on to the pub or restaurant that is the rendezvous of the particular club. Each club has, quite unofficially, its own place where members from the various teams congregate on Saturday evenings to discuss each other's doings over a mixed grill and many pints of ale. No distinction is made there between the member of the first XV who is in the running for his 'cap' and the eighth forward of an extra 'C'. The rugger world is a family party. Some do the thing better than others; that is all there is to it. And so the evening passes till the bar is closed, the gathering is dispersed, and the other world resumes its hold on one, till the following Wednesday will bring from the team secretary the yellow card 'You are selected to play v. — 1.15 Waterloo, meet 1.5 at barrier', and Saturday afternoon sees the same innumerable musters before the same innumerable platforms.

And so, and so . . . on every Saturday from the end of September till the end of March, except on that Saturday when there is no rugger in London because everyone will be at Twickenham; on every Saturday till one is forced to quit the ranks of those that play for those that must sit on committees and shout from the touch line and exhort the young.

That is the rugger world. The best of all possible worlds? . . . There be those that find it so.

A Winter's Tale

JOHN DANN

John Dann eloquently catalogues the reasons why people enjoy rugby.
From *Kicked Into Touch: The Life and Times of
Thomas Cook's Amateur Rugby Club 1910–1966* (2011).

❧

IMAGINE THE SCENE if you will. It's a winter's Saturday afternoon, the sound of voices – it's the buzz of good-natured banter from a crowded changing room. You are part of the team, tying up the final lace knot on your boots, catching that familiar smell of leather and Dubbin. Then filing out (with perhaps a friendly pat for *Brigitte*), along the corridors echoing to the clatter of many studs, with team-mates to the pitch. The anticipation of a new game – running up and down on the spot and the 'butterflies' before 'kick-off', getting your tackle in first (memories of 'scythe them down'). Taking a hit, releasing a team-mate to carry the ball, or the sheer joy of receiving and holding a pass – beating your man and running towards the line, ball in hands (there is no greater exhilaration known to man). The welcome half-time oranges (perhaps a 'snifter' or smoke for the non-conformists), a group huddle, the captain's view of the game and individual performances so far (expletives deleted). Instinctively standing in line sportingly clapping our visitors – win or lose, into the Ravensbourne clubhouse with a friendly pat or two. At an away match receiving applause in turn (slightly embarrassed) from opponents on their home ground. Their hospitality too, occasionally providing half-pints of shandies, waiting for us in the changing room, to be gratefully downed in one (with a theatrical belch from some). Staring vacantly at the floor strewn with clots of studded earth, sitting exhausted, on the benches under a row of hooks on which limply hangs an assortment of our togs. Wincing at some yet undiscovered injury and sensing the lingering medicated smell of wintergreen. The shaking hands and limited speech from physical effort followed by the examinations of a swollen lip or cut eye. Someone pulls out a packet of 'gaspers', reaching out for a (cadged) Players cigarette enjoying long pulls and exhaling at leisure. The steaming shirts heaped on the changing room floor, the shouts from the showers (especially if lukewarm or cold) and the bliss of jumping naked into a steaming hot plunge bath. Afterwards, freshly scrubbed (with the lingering scent of Wright's coal tar soap), into the bar. Glass mug in hand (held by the bowl – never the handle) anticipating the contents of the enamel beer jug, as it moves methodically on its pilgrimage around the team towards you. Marvelling and watching the sexy young girls the opposition clubhouses seemed to attract. The songs (learning new verses), social camaraderie, the sense of belonging, and the exquisite thought that this experience will repeat itself all over again – next Saturday.

And perhaps you still cannot fathom why boys and men do this, then, your answer is, as the French rugby enthusiast Pierre de Coubertin, said, 'In order to understand and appreciate it fully, one must have played it . . . this beautiful sport.'

A Fascinating Game

W. ROWE HARDING

In the final pages of *Rugby Reminiscences and Opinions* (1929), Harding, then a recently retired Welsh international and later a Circuit Court judge and part of the Welsh sporting establishment, puts the case for considering rugby an art form and a source of its own kind of aesthetic experience.

RUGBY IS A fascinating game, how fascinating the mere spectators never know. The pleasure of doing things is infinitely greater than the pleasure of seeing things done. I have always felt annoyed at the attitude of two types of person. The one is the man who cannot tolerate the non-athlete, and the other is the non-athlete who cannot tolerate the athlete. The non-athlete is the more blameworthy, since it must be presumed that his pleasures are the pleasures of the mind. Reflection should teach him that athletics do not appeal to him because he has not the right type of muscle for quick and graceful movement. A man with bow legs and a club foot cannot possibly get any joy out of running, nor can the ordinary man whose running efforts are restricted to catching buses and trains; but a man with a figure like that of Douglas Lowe, with supple limbs and quick muscles, gets a thrill out of running which men of less graceful mould cannot possibly experience. A cart horse may derive a heavy delight from pulling a dray up a hill, but he cannot enjoy running a mile at a gallop in the same way as a thoroughbred racehorse enjoys it. The man who sneers at rugby merely because he does not enjoy playing it himself is bigoted, and the man who cannot see beauty in rugby is blind. It is a profound if trite saying that beauty lies in the eye of the beholder. Some spectators watch rugby because they want to see their own side win, and others because they like to see quick movement; but the finest and most subtle attractions of the game can be discerned only by the keen vision of intelligence.

That is why rugby holds its place over soccer in the affections of Public Schools and Varsities. Soccer is popular because it is easily understood, its good qualities are apparent on the surface. Juggling tricks amuse the mind of the child because their cleverness is apparent. A deeper insight and knowledge is necessary fully to appreciate rugby. The discipline of a well-drilled pack may escape the observation of a superficial observer, the complicated processes essential to a quick heel from the scrum can only be appreciated by the careful and intelligent observer. The art of playing rugby is inferior to the higher art forms, only because the necessary technique for the higher forms of art can only be acquired by long study and perseverance. A certain amount of concentration and perseverance is necessary in rugby, but to excel at the game natural ability is ninety per cent of the battle. In music, literature and painting natural ability is only half the battle; hard work is the other half, and therein alone lies the superior merit of the successful artist. I very much doubt, however, if the artist gets any keener delight out of his art than the rugby player gets out of his rugby.

For my part I would not exchange my aesthetic experiences in rugby for those of any painter, singer or writer, because they are, after all, merely concerned with symbols. The singer has a fuller self-expression than the painter, but even he is merely acting a part. The rugby player during the course of a game is living life at its most intoxicating. There is movement, energy, grace, strength, fear, intelligence, competition, everything. When our economists have settled the problems of living, what remains but to live? And living gets its fullest expression when every nerve and fibre of body and brain is at high tension.

Like all fascinating things, however, rugby has its dangers. It is essentially a game for the young and above all for the fit. To say that rugby is good for the health is wrong. It is played above the natural pace of living and imposes a tremendous strain upon every organ in the body, and the weakest go to the wall. It is a pitiless searcher-out of lurking constitutional weaknesses. So many of the greatest exponents of rugby have fallen into an early grave. It does not necessarily follow because a man is a good athlete that he is robust and sound organically. Indeed, the best athletes are often delicate human mechanisms which break down beyond repair at the smallest over-exertion. One cannot but be struck by the large number of famous rugby players who died untimely deaths.

The life of a rugby player is therefore a dangerous one. He runs graver risks for the sake of sport than almost any athlete. For that reason he should not delay his retirement too long, because rugby is no game for old bones. When he does retire he must seek other forms of exercise less strenuous, but exercise of some kind he must have. His body has been trained up to expect it, and if he does not get it he becomes lazy, flabby and old before his time. Those are the dangers which attend the rugby player. I have no doubt the ardent rugby player will consider them, weigh them carefully, and decide the game is worth the risk because it is the greatest of all winter games. Whether it is a greater game than cricket I take leave of my rugby friends to doubt, but certainly no other game than cricket teaches as many excellent qualities and gives such full-blooded pleasure as the game of rugby.

Now, after ten years, I feel as others have felt before, that I am only beginning to learn the game (an opinion shared by my critics), and that nature is unkind to deprive my legs of their speed when my mind is active and as keen as ever. Of course there are other pleasant things in life, and in a year or two I shall have acquired another point of view and found other pleasures; but, although I have tasted other pleasures, I have drunk deeply of one, of the pleasures of the game of rugby, and it has been to me, as to thousands of others, the best thing in life. It can become an obsession, and that is the danger I would warn young players against. I have known men whose whole life was sacrificed to rugby, who played it until they were middle-aged, who refused to give it up before their health gave way. Their only literature was rugby literature, their only interest in life was rugby. They knew in the end that their life would not be a long one, and that it was sacrificed to rugby football, but they neither complained nor regretted it. Nevertheless, of course, they were lives thrown away, and it is as well that rugby players should know the risks that attend excessive enthusiasm. Now that one's playing days are over, two things only are left: memory, and the friendships of one's contemporaries. In the end they are the things which make the game worthwhile.

Acknowledgements

We are grateful for permission to include extracts from the following copyright work:

Denzil Batchelor: *Babbled of Green Fields* (Hutchinson, 1961), reproduced by permission of The Random House Group Ltd and David Higham Associates for the author.

Richard Beard: *Muddied Oafs* (Yellow Jersey, 2003), copyright © Richard Beard 2003, reproduced by permission of The Random House Group Ltd.

Derek Bevan: *The Man in the Middle* (Seren, 2001), reproduced by permission of the publisher.

Peter Bills: *Jean-Pierre Rives: A Modern Corinthian* (Allen & Unwin, 1986), copyright © Peter Bills 1986, reproduced by permission of HarperCollins Publishers Ltd.

Nick Bishop and Alun Carter: *The Good, The Bad and the Ugly: The Rise and Fall of Pontypool RFC* (Mainstream, 2013), reproduced by permission of The Random House Group Ltd.

Kenneth R Bogle: *Walter Sutherland: Scottish Rugby Legend 1890-1918* (Tempus, 2005), copyright © Kenneth R Bogle 2005, reproduced by permission of the author.

Eddie Butler: *The Greatest Welsh XV Ever* (Gomer, 2011), reproduced by permission of Gomer Press Ltd.

Tony Collins: *A Social History of English Rugby Union* (Routledge, 2009), copyright © Routledge 2009, reproduced by permission of Taylor & Francis Books UK.

James Corsan: *For Poulton and England: The Life and Times of an Edwardian Rugby Hero* (Matador, 2009), reproduced by permission of the author.

John Dann: *Kicked Into Touch: The Life and Times of Thomas Cook's Amateur Club 1910-1966* (Fastprint, 2010), reproduced by permission of the author.

Colin Deans: *You're a Hooker, Then: An Autobiography* (Mainstream, 1987), reproduced by permission of the author.

Philip Dine: *French Rugby Football: A Cultural History* (Berg, 2001), copyright © Philip Dine 2001, reproduced by permission of Berg Publishers, an imprint of Bloomsbury Publishing Plc.

Steven Gauge: *My Life as a Hooker* (Summersdale, 2012), reproduced by permission of Summersdale Publishers Ltd.

James Gilbert: from a talk given in the 1940s, 'Rugby Footballs in the making', reproduced by permission of Gilbert Rugby.

Rowe Harding: *Rugby Reminiscences and Opinions* (Pilot Press, 1929), reproduced by permission of the heirs of Rowe Harding.

Gavin Hastings with Clem Thomas: *High Balls and Happy Hours* (Mainstream, 1994), reproduced by permission of the publishers, The Random House Group Ltd, and the author.

Mick Imlah: 'London Scottish (1914)' from *The Lost Leader* (Faber, 2008), reproduced by permission of Faber & Faber Ltd and Mark Ford for the Estate of Mick Imlah.

Frank Keating: *Up and Under: a rugby diary* (Hodder & Stoughton, 1983), copyright © Frank Keating 1983, reproduced by permission of Hodder & Stoughton Ltd.

Mark Keohane: *Chester: A Biography of Courage* (Don Nelson, 2001), reproduced by permission of the author.

Chris Laidlaw: *Mud in Your Eye* (Pelham Books, 1973), copyright © Chris Laidlaw 1973, reproduced by permission of the author.

Michael Latham: *Buff Berry and the Mighty Bongers* (Mike R. L. Publications, 1995), reproduced by permission of the author.

Robert Lynd: *The Goldfish* (Methuen, 1927), reproduced by permission of Tim Wheeler for the Estate of Robert Lynd.

Willie John McBride and Peter Bills: *Willie John: The Story of My Life* (Portrait/Piatkus, 2004), reproduced by permission of the publishers, Little Brown Book Group Ltd.

Roger McGough: 'Big Arth' from *Sporting Relations* (Penguin, 1997),copyright © Roger McGough 1974, 1997, reproduced by permission of United Agents (www.unitedagents.co.uk) on behalf of Roger McGough.

Jennifer Macrory: *Running with the Ball: The Birth of Rugby Football* (Collins Willow, 1991), copyright © Jennifer Macrory 1991, reproduced by permission of HarperCollins Publishers Ltd.

Ron Mitchell: *So Why Did You Become a Referee?* (Mitchell, 2004), reproduced by permission of the author.

Brian Moore: *Beware of the Dog: Rugby's Hard Man Reveals All* (Simon & Schuster, 2010), reproduced by permission of Simon & Schuster Ltd.

Sue Mott: *A Girl's Guide to Ball Games: What Men Need to Know* (Mainstream, 1996), reproduced by permission of the publishers, The Random House Group Ltd.

Graham Mourie with Ron Palenski: *Graham Mourie: Captain* (Arthur Barker, 1982), reproduced by permission Graham Mourie.

George Nepia and Terry McLean: *I George Nepia: The Autobiography of a Rugby Legend* (London League, 2002), reproduced by permission of London League Publications Ltd.

Brian O'Driscoll: *A Year in the Centre* (Penguin 2005), copyright © Brian O'Driscoll 2005, reproduced by permission of Penguin Books Ltd.

Jeff Probyn and Barry Newcombe: *Upfront: The Jeff Probyn Story* (Mainstream, 1994), reproduced by permission of the publishers, The Random House Group Ltd, and the author.

John Reason and Carwyn Jones: *The World of Rugby* (BBC Books, 1979), reproduced by permission of the publishers, The Random House Group Ltd, and Mrs Joan Reason.

Huw Richards: *A Game for Hooligans: The History of Rugby Union* (Mainstream, 2006), reproduced by permission of the publishers, The Random House Group Ltd.

Tom Salmon: *The First Hundred Years* (CRFU, 1983), copyright © CRFU 1983, reproduced by permission of the Cornwall Rugby Football Union.

J. C. Squire: 'The Rugger Match', privately published in 1922, reproduced by permission of Roger Squire.

J. B. G. Thomas: *Great Rugger Players* (Stanley Paul, 1955), reproduced by permission of Wayne Thomas.

Alex Veysey: *Colin Meads: All Black* (Collins, 1974), reproduced by permission of HarperCollins Publishers (New Zealand) Ltd.

Phil Vickery with Alison Kervin: *Raging Bull: The Autobiography of the English Rugby Legend* (HarperSport, 2010), copyright © Philip Vickery 2010, reproduced by permission of HarperCollins Publishers Ltd.

Philip Warner: The Harlequins (Breedon Books, 1991), copyright © Philip Warner 1991, reproduced by permission of JMD Media Ltd.

Alec Waugh: from 'The Young Man's Game' in *On Doing What One Likes* (Cayme Press, 1926), reprinted by permission of Peters Fraser & Dunlop (www.petersfraserdunlop.com) on behalf of the Estate of Alexander Waugh.

J. P. R. Williams with Miles Harrison: *JPR: Given the Breaks: My Life in Rugby* (Hodder & Stoughton, 2006), copyright © J. P. R. Williams 2006, reproduced by permission of Hodder & Stoughton Ltd.

P. G. Wodehouse: 'The Great Day', copyright © P. G. Wodehouse 1913, first published in *London Opinion and The Alleynian*, March 1913, reproduced by permission of the Estate of the author, c/o Rogers Coleridge & White Ltd, 20 Powis Mews, London W11 1JN.

Every effort has been made to trace and contact copyright holders. If there are any inadvertent omissions we apologise to those concerned, and ask that you contact us so that we can correct any oversight as soon as possible.

Index